D0464191

Praise for *The Other 80 Percent*

"I can't believe the amount of research that Thumma and Bird put into this project. I immediately began to give renewed focus to some areas that our church's leadership had let slide. It contains so much practical stuff that I am going to make sure our ministry teams read and apply the strategic practices of *The Other 80 Percent*."

—Dr. Michael Slaughter, lead pastor, Ginghamsburg
Church; author, *Change the World: Recovering
the Mission and Message of Jesus*

"This book is what you get when a researcher and a pragmatic team up to address a critical topic in the life of congregations. It will not only help you understand why your members are not more involved, it will help you do something about it! This is one of those rare books that could come with a money-back guarantee. If you are not better equipped to reengage the less-involved members of your congregation after reading this book, I will be shocked. Any single chapter of this book is worth the full price. Never has so much solid material been packed into one book on a topic seldom addressed in the life of congregations."

—Dr. C. Jeff Woods, American Baptist Churches, USA

"Over and again I hear from clergy about the challenge of getting their members involved. Thumma and Bird have done the hard work and provided the answer to this ages-old dilemma. In this superb volume, you find plenty of hard data, lots of practical suggestions, and an entire program that can transform a congregation. An absolutely essential read for any clergy who wants to find the way forward."

—Rev. Ian S. Markham, Ph.D., dean and president,
Virginia Theological Seminary, Alexandria, VA

"I love this book. Thumma and Bird love the church enough to call us on our sloppy thinking, hunches, and outdated assumptions, and they have the expertise to present us with the facts. Their thorough research forces us to listen to the people we never hear from, the people on the outskirts of church, the ones who have left or may be about to. God is still speaking, even through that disengaged 80 percent who may not want to stay that way, if only we will learn from what they have to say."

—Rev. Dr. Lillian Daniel, senior minister, First
Congregational Church, United Church of Christ;
author, *This Odd and Wondrous Calling:
The Public and Private Lives of Two Ministers*

The Other 80 Percent

TURNING YOUR CHURCH'S
SPECTATORS INTO *Active* PARTICIPANTS

Scott Thumma
and Warren Bird

JOSSEY-BASS
A Wiley Imprint
www.josseybass.com

A **Leadership✖Network** Publication

Published by Jossey-Bass
A Wiley Imprint
989 Market Street, San Francisco, CA 94103-1741—www.josseybass.com

Scripture quotations marked (NIV) are taken from the Holy Bible, New International Version®, NIV®. Copyright © 1973, 1978, 1984 by Biblica, Inc.™ Used by permission of Zondervan. All rights reserved worldwide. www.zondervan.com

Scripture quotations marked NLT are taken from the Holy Bible, New Living Translation, copyright 1996, 2004. Used by permission of Tyndale House Publishers, Inc., Wheaton, Illinois 60189. All rights reserved.

Jossey-Bass also publishes its books in a variety of electronic formats. Some content that appears in print may not be available in electronic books.

Library of Congress Cataloging-in-Publication Data

Thumma, Scott.
    The other 80 percent : turning your church's spectators into active participants / Scott Thumma, Warren Bird.
        p.   cm.— (Jossey-bass leadership network series ; 56)
    Includes bibliographical references and index.
    ISBN 978-0-470-89129-2 (hardback); 978-1-118-02534-5 (ebk); 978-1-118-02535-2 (ebk); 978-1-118-02536-9 (ebk)
        1. Discipling (Christianity)   2. Pastoral theology—Protestant churches.   I. Bird, Warren. II. Title.
    BV4520.T58 2011
    253—dc22
                                                                                2010053856

Printed in the United States of America
FIRST EDITION
HB Printing   10 9 8 7 6 5 4 3 2 1

Leadership Network Titles

The Blogging Church: Sharing the Story of Your Church Through Blogs, Brian
    Bailey and Terry Storch
Church Turned Inside Out: A Guide for Designers, Refiners, and Re-Aligners,
    Linda Bergquist and Allan Karr
*Leading from the Second Chair: Serving Your Church, Fulfilling Your Role, and
    Realizing Your Dreams*, Mike Bonem and Roger Patterson
Hybrid Church: The Fusion of Intimacy and Impact, Dave Browning
The Way of Jesus: A Journey of Freedom for Pilgrims and Wanderers, Jonathan
    S. Campbell with Jennifer Campbell
*Cracking Your Church's Culture Code: Seven Keys to Unleashing Vision and
    Inspiration*, Samuel R. Chand
*Leading the Team-Based Church: How Pastors and Church Staffs Can Grow
    Together into a Powerful Fellowship of Leaders*, George Cladis
Organic Church: Growing Faith Where Life Happens, Neil Cole
Church 3.0: Upgrades for the Future of the Church, Neil Cole
Journeys to Significance: Charting a Leadership Course from the Life of Paul,
    Neil Cole
Off-Road Disciplines: Spiritual Adventures of Missional Leaders, Earl Creps
*Reverse Mentoring: How Young Leaders Can Transform the Church and Why
    We Should Let Them*, Earl Creps
*Building a Healthy Multi-Ethnic Church: Mandate, Commitments, and Practices
    of a Diverse Congregation*, Mark DeYmaz
Leading Congregational Change Workbook, James H. Furr, Mike Bonem, and
    Jim Herrington
The Tangible Kingdom: Creating Incarnational Community, Hugh Halter and
    Matt Smay
*Baby Boomers and Beyond: Tapping the Ministry Talents and Passions of Adults
    over Fifty*, Amy Hanson
*Leading Congregational Change: A Practical Guide for the Transformational
    Journey*, Jim Herrington, Mike Bonem, and James H. Furr

The Leader's Journey: Accepting the Call to Personal and Congregational Transformation, Jim Herrington, Robert Creech, and Trisha Taylor

Whole Church: Leading from Fragmentation to Engagement, Mel Lawrenz

Culture Shift: Transforming Your Church from the Inside Out, Robert Lewis and Wayne Cordeiro, with Warren Bird

Church Unique: How Missional Leaders Cast Vision, Capture Culture, and Create Movement, Will Mancini

A New Kind of Christian: A Tale of Two Friends on a Spiritual Journey, Brian D. McLaren

The Story We Find Ourselves In: Further Adventures of a New Kind of Christian, Brian D. McLaren

Missional Renaissance: Changing the Scorecard for the Church, Reggie McNeal

Practicing Greatness: 7 Disciplines of Extraordinary Spiritual Leaders, Reggie McNeal

The Present Future: Six Tough Questions for the Church, Reggie McNeal

A Work of Heart: Understanding How God Shapes Spiritual Leaders, Reggie McNeal

The Millennium Matrix: Reclaiming the Past, Reframing the Future of the Church, M. Rex Miller

Your Church in Rhythm: The Forgotten Dimensions of Seasons and Cycles, Bruce B. Miller

Shaped by God's Heart: The Passion and Practices of Missional Churches, Milfred Minatrea

The Missional Leader: Equipping Your Church to Reach a Changing World, Alan J. Roxburgh and Fred Romanuk

Missional Map-Making: Skills for Leading in Times of Transition, Alan J. Roxburgh

Relational Intelligence: How Leaders Can Expand Their Influence Through a New Way of Being Smart, Steve Saccone

Viral Churches: Helping Church Planters Become Movement Makers, Ed Stetzer and Warren Bird

The Externally Focused Quest: Becoming the Best Church for the Community, Eric Swanson and Rick Rusaw

The Ascent of a Leader: How Ordinary Relationships Develop Extraordinary Character and Influence, Bill Thrall, Bruce McNicol, and Ken McElrath

Beyond Megachurch Myths: What We Can Learn from America's Largest Churches, Scott Thumma and Dave Travis

The Other 80 Percent: Turning Your Church's Spectators into Active Participants, Scott Thumma and Warren Bird

The Elephant in the Boardroom: Speaking the Unspoken About Pastoral Transitions, Carolyn Weese and J. Russell Crabtree

Contents

Tables and Figures

About the Jossey-Bass Leadership Network Series

Leadership Network's mission is to accelerate the impact of OneHundredX leaders. These high-capacity leaders are like the hundredfold crop that comes from seed planted in good soil as Jesus described in Matthew 13:8.

Leadership Network . . .

- explores the "what's next?" of what could be.
- creates "aha!" environments for collaborative discovery.
- works with exceptional "positive deviants."
- invests in the success of others through generous relationships.
- pursues big impact through measurable kingdom results.
- strives to model Jesus through all we do.

Believing that meaningful conversations and strategic connections can change the world, we seek to help leaders navigate the future by exploring new ideas and finding application for each unique context. Through collaborative meetings and processes, leaders map future possibilities and challenge one another to action that accelerates fruitfulness and effectiveness. Leadership Network shares the learnings and inspiration with others through our books, concept papers, research reports, e-newsletters, podcasts, videos, and online experiences. This in turn generates a ripple effect of new conversations and further influence.

In 1996 Leadership Network established a partnership with Jossey-Bass, a Wiley Imprint, to develop a series of creative books that provide thought leadership to innovators in church ministry. Leadership Network Publications present thoroughly researched and innovative concepts from leading thinkers, practitioners, and pioneering churches.

Leadership Network is a division of OneHundredX, a global ministry with initiatives around the world.

To learn more about Leadership Network, go to www.leadnet.org

To learn more about OneHundredX, go to www.100x.org

Preface

How can you shift more of your church members from sitting to serving, from being spectators to engaging more deeply? Would doing so help more people to grow and develop spiritually?

Virtually every church in America faces this same problem. While participation percentages may vary from church to church, the core challenge does not: What will motivate less-connected or less-active members to move toward a life of discipleship and of living out the faith in community?

Our title is *The Other 80 Percent* because your church—unless it's extremely unusual—has far too many people who are willing to let 20 percent of the membership engage in most of the church's work. Perhaps some are "underinvolved." Others are minimally active. Some are total spectators. Still others don't even come to church and yet are on the membership roster. Whatever the case, we want to show you specific ways that can move many of these other 80 percent onto pathways of participation, engagement, and community—and hopefully also more fulfilling spiritual lives.

This book can help you address that challenge in very practical ways. Its insights apply whether your attendance is fifty, five hundred, or five thousand—since "bystanders" are present in churches of every size. Further there are nonparticipants in old churches and new. They identify with denominational churches and independent ones. They are associated with white, black, Asian, Hispanic, and multiethnic churches too. They cover the spectrum theologically from liberal to conservative. It seems that no one is exempt.

In the Trenches

This book started during a marathon of church visits. We selected twelve churches and asked if they'd let us study them from the inside out. Typically the two of us (Scott from Connecticut, Warren from New York) would fly to a given city on a Saturday. We'd rent a car and visit our designated church through Wednesday. We joined the worship services, dropped in on Sunday schools or other Sunday ministries, toured the facilities, conducted an all-church survey, and most of all interviewed lots of people. We followed the same process at all twelve churches.

We had a lot of fun during random conversations as well as through our structured focus groups. At each church one focus group was with newcomers; another was with long-term members; a third, with lay leaders; and a fourth, with the leadership staff. We also interviewed the senior pastor and various staff members. Our overall task was to ask: Why do people choose this church? How do they get involved? How do they grow spiritually?

Many of the stories we tell in this book come from those Scott-and-Warren church visits. Some are comical, such as the newcomer's unsuccessful quest to "find the special gift" one church had promised to its guests. Others are inspiring, such as the man in a Christ-centered recovery group who announced, "With God's help I've been cocaine-free for one hundred days," followed by enthusiastic applause. Some stories are sad, mostly those of people explaining why they disengaged from church. Some are hopeful, including our closing testimonial from a dropout who came back to his church.

What we learned was eye-opening. It wasn't what we expected. In many cases, what the staff told us was nothing like the actual process people experienced in getting involved at their churches. Our approach seemed so basic: find out why people engage and participate, and also find out about the people who attend church but aren't otherwise involved. But in following this approach, we found a wealth of surprising discoveries.

"We've got to tell people what we're learning," we decided. "It will help other churches, since all of them deal with this same issue."

This need to voice what we had learned was even more apparent as we interacted with pastors from small and midsized churches, whether mainline or Evangelical. The concern about low participation was continually echoed in Scott's interactions with doctor of ministry students and for both of us in our teaching of seminary students. Many of these students and pastors expressed over and again the challenge of trying to get busy, overcommitted members involved in the life of the congregation and active in the faith. "What do I have to do to get more people involved? Why do so few of my members show up? Why don't people want to get on board?" we heard. "Why are people's commitments so low?"

These experiences and insights led to what became this book, which draws from our research as well as that of others. In fact a unique quality of this book is that it draws on the analysis of several major national research projects (which are further described in Appendix B) in order to cross-check patterns that arose in our own data. In the national surveys and interviews over one hundred thousand people described their involvement level at church. Our goal in drawing from what church members said in interviews and surveys is to show you what will help move spectators and marginal participants to a more active commitment and to a robust life of discipleship. And we hope to give church leaders in other congregations an approach and research-derived suggestions to do the same.

Walk-Through

In the Introduction we open this journey with a parable about a shepherd and a flock of sheep to raise some of the questions that we've been pondering in our research. The parable also sets the tone for the book. We are dealing with a very real problem, and we provide here a positive, practical, and hopeful spirit to confront it. We also describe a process to address this challenge.

We divide the bulk of the book into three parts: Listening, Learning, and Leading. Part One, "Listening," reports on a lot of listening we did. It goes on to show you how to create a *listening team*. We describe what we learned when we listened to the roughly 20 percent who seem to do everything in the typical church (Chapter One), and also to the roughly 80 percent who are less committed (Chapter Two). Then we show how you can give attention to the voices in your own congregation—those affiliated with your church at a variety of levels (Chapter Three).

Part Two, "Learning," moves from the individual to a broader perspective, concluding with a very practical approach on how to create a *learning team*. We look at issues in the greater culture (Chapter Four), at the distinctive qualities of church such as its theology and size and patterns of volunteer development (Chapter Five), and at the sometimes faulty and limiting perspectives leaders have about how people increase their involvement (Chapter Six). The final chapter of this part (Chapter Seven) shows how you too can reap similar learnings from your own church and community by establishing a learning team.

Part Three, "Leading," suggests the next steps for your church's leadership team. You'll learn ways to build on your existing momentum by accelerating what you're already doing to engage your members (Chapter Eight). We'll also suggest how you can creatively enlarge on what it means for people to engage and take part with their church (Chapter Nine). Our final chapter (Chapter Ten) reinforces the idea that spiritual growth and development are directly related to participation and involvement, and that the spiritual development of the entire congregation should be the motivation for this effort. This speaks to the ultimate goal of the book: building the spiritual life of your entire flock, including "the other 80 percent."

The Afterword offers a new sheep parable, hinting at an ideal outcome of applying the lessons of this book. We also offer supplemental material in an annotated bibliography and in appendixes containing suggested resources and descriptions of our research and the datasets we have drawn from.

What matters most, and what we underscore throughout the book, is the creation of a community of active disciples of Jesus Christ—not disengaged "church members" who while seldom participating in church want their names to be on some sacred roll for the time when they are "called up yonder," as the old song goes.

If you are like most church leaders, you aren't satisfied with the status quo of so many uninvolved people associated with your church. "It shouldn't be this way," something tells you. You want to engage the less-active portion of your congregation at a higher level. You do care about the other 80 percent, or whatever the exact percentage is for your church. Indeed the same core problem faces every church: What will motivate the more disconnected attenders to move farther along into discipleship and living out the faith in community?

If that is your question or dream, please turn the page. . . .

Introduction

Wandering Sheep

And he gathered his disciples around him, and taught them saying:
There was a shepherd tending his flock. One evening during his
count he discovered that one sheep from his flock of one hundred had
gone astray, and was missing. "Not to worry," he thought, "I still
have ninety-nine. Their wool will sustain me and my family. After
all, the missing sheep was not so productive anyway."

In the morning he led the remaining sheep to a familiar green
pasture. Several sheep were tired of the same grass, the same bub-
bling brook, and the same weekly routine, so they decided to wander
over the knoll and off to another seemingly greener meadow dotted
with buttercups and clover. The shepherd called out to them, but they
didn't heed his pleas. His faithful border collie attempted to round up
the errant members of the flock to no avail. After a while the shep-
herd whistled to the collie, saying, "Come on back. They will return
on their own this evening. If not, I'm sure some other shepherd will
find them and care for them."

Over the coming weeks a few of the wayward sheep returned.
But a few more also wandered off, following the norm set by others.
Perhaps they assumed that the other pastures must be pleasant indeed
since so few of their friends had returned. Perhaps they simply did not
want to participate regularly with a flock. Whenever the shepherd saw
them, he invited them back, but eventually he gave up. "They'll come
if they're hungry," he decided.

When shearing day arrived, the flock had dwindled to just forty-
two. A dozen had amounts of wool that were quite unproductive
and were hardly worth shearing. Ten were still lambs and needed

their undeveloped wool coats to survive the cold evenings. Thus the shepherd sheared the remaining twenty productive sheep, bagged their wool, and took it to market.

On the way home the shepherd thought about the twenty sheep that had developed healthy wool coats. He pondered why his total flock hadn't been more productive this year and how his family would survive on his meager income. "Perhaps," he thought, "if I could just entice some sheep from my neighbor's flock to join my flock, then all would be well. Or maybe I can find a few of the remaining wild rams on the mountainside."

So off he went to try.

● ● ●

In the real parable the shepherd is troubled to lose even one sheep. He looks until he finds the one that was lost, and brings it back to rejoin the other ninety-nine (Luke 15:1–7). In the spirit of that idea, this book could have been titled *The Other 1 Percent.*

Do you think the church you serve could come significantly closer to the parable's ideal of 99 percent being present and active? Take a minute to ponder what your church would look like if 99 percent of your flock were fully engaged—heart, mind, soul, and strength. Can you imagine every role filled by people who really want to be there? What if the names in every volunteer position represented people who excite you with their passion and new ideas for ministry?

Carry these imaginings a bit further. What if you had more leaders than existing ministry slots? What if those leaders, in turn, didn't lack for volunteers to serve with them? What if virtually all of those people were being discipled through a healthy small-group system in your church? What if almost everyone associated with your church put God first in their finances and gave generously?

The message of *The Other 80 Percent* is this: *If you pay attention to your less-involved people, they will become more involved.* We want to show you how to do that on the basis of what people just like them told us. We know that greater involvement does not guarantee the ultimate goal of greater spiritual growth, but we also know that the two go together quite often. More specifically, research on churches shows that the greater the percentage of engaged members, the more likely the church is to be vital, thriving, and spiritually healthy. This book can show you ways to move a far greater percentage of your flock in that direction.

Who Brought Pareto to Church?

Our goal is to help you reverse the pattern implied in the title of the book: the commonly noted observation that 20 percent of the people in a church do 80 percent of the work. We also want to challenge the implicit assumption that the 20 percent deserve all of your focus while the other 80 percent can be left largely alone until that hoped-for day when they sort things out on their own accord and take the initiative to become involved.

This 80/20 concept is a version of the "Pareto Principle," a rule of thumb derived from observations made by Vilfredo Pareto, an Italian economist, at the turn of the twentieth century. He realized in researching the distribution of wealth in Italy that the pattern of distribution showed an uneven relationship. The vast majority of wealth was concentrated in relatively few holdings. Specifically, in 1906, 80 percent of the land in Italy was owned by 20 percent of the population. This distributive principle, also commonly known today as the 80/20 rule or the "law of the vital few," can be seen to hold true across many sectors of society. To state the principle in other words, the majority of results come from a minority of the efforts. For example:

- In business, 20 percent of one's clients typically generate 80 percent of one's sales.
- The richest 20 percent of the world's population controls roughly 80 percent of the world's income.

- In computer science, by fixing the top 20 percent of the most reported bugs, 80 percent of errors and crashes can be eliminated.
- In U.S. health care, 20 percent of patients use 80 percent of health care resources.
- Several criminology studies have found that 20 percent of the criminals commit 80 percent of the crimes.

And in the church world, a handful of members typically account for most of the effort in the congregation. (Additionally, a few of the parishioners cause most of the headaches!)

We believe the Pareto Principle is an observed and accepted pattern of behavior, but not an immutable law of nature for churches. It may happen that roughly 20 percent of your congregation is active while roughly 80 percent too often stand on the margins, but it does not have to be so.

Likewise certain assumptions follow from this idea—particularly in the world of business. They suggest that to maximize revenue with a minimum of effort or cost, you should focus on your best customers, appeal to your wealthiest clients, and reward your hardest workers, since it is with these that you will reap the greatest results for the least effort. This makes perfect sense if your goal is to minimize cost and maximize profit, that is, to get the most bang per buck.

The biblical standard for kingdom ventures is different. Churches are not for-profit ventures. We don't want to sacrifice the ideal of 100 percent engagement and involvement in order to keep effort or costs down.

Nowhere in Scripture are two different levels of participation encouraged—the 20 percent and the 80 percent—for those who follow Jesus. In fact Jesus has strong words for any of us who say one thing and do another, or who follow him halfheartedly.

Likewise God's call to church leaders is to watch over the entire flock, not just 20 percent of it. God holds church leaders responsible for the spiritual development of their flock. Hebrews 13:17 says this about their charge: "Their work is to watch over your souls, and they will give an account of their care of you to God" (NLT). Is it acceptable to neglect the one sheep that strayed, to allow the widow's mite to remain lost, or to write off the prodigal son rather than longing for him to return and rejoicing when he does?

> God holds church leaders responsible for the spiritual development of their flock.... Is it acceptable to neglect the one sheep that strayed?

The answer, obviously, is no! Each child, young person, and adult is precious in God's sight, and should be nurtured and matured in our churches.

Balancing Act

To increase involvement in your church, you will need to move in directions you might not have previously considered. Granted, Jesus' parable, where only one sheep out of ninety-nine is wayward or lost, is a far cry from the reality found in most of America's churches. Certainly no pastor or church leadership team intentionally wants to exclude or overlook persons who belong to their churches—barring moments of frustration with a Grumpy Gus or Divisive Dora. Nor do clergy and lay leaders explicitly make decisions to ignore those in their midst who are uninvolved, marginal, or are drifting toward inactivity.

Actually there is a third type of person in this equation. Besides "more active" and "less active" people (categories we will define in the first two chapters), you also have totally new people. Church leaders certainly don't want their efforts at bringing in new persons to dissipate their attention toward those who are already present. Yet we know we need to reach out and bring new people into the congregation if we are to fulfill Jesus' mandates in Matthew 28:19–20 and elsewhere to make disciples of all nations (much less to survive).

We assume you have a solid theology that values reaching lost people and providing spiritual nurture to those who have been reached. However, if all the church's attention focuses on outreach and first-timer hospitality, will that not rob from the church's energy, efforts, and resources toward those already attending?

Many books are written these days that assist a church in how to reach out and invite newcomers, and then offer them hospitality and integration into the church. We're fully in favor of that practice (the Annotated Bibliography lists several good books on the subject). This book focuses on another big issue, an equally pressing need in many of America's churches: how to understand and motivate the marginal people already associated with your congregation. *The Other 80 Percent* offers strategies for reshaping the church's systems and volunteer structures in an effort to address the needs of marginal participants, hopefully moving them toward more active involvement.

Furthermore we are not suggesting anything here that would sidetrack the development and deeper maturation of existing saints. Indeed this is the balancing act that all leaders are faced with: how to maintain equilibrium between outreach and what might be called "inreach." You want to give attention to potential participants, but you also want to offer continued discipleship to the existing congregation. This latter group includes not only your regulars but also your more inactive folks.

It is not that pastors lack awareness of those who slip out the back door and join the ranks of the detached and disinterested members of our churches. But the process is often gradual. Sometimes the church's efforts and primary focus on welcoming newcomers and involving its more responsive people can hinder its need to track and recall those who are gradually drifting away.

What Causes This Problem?

The current general malaise in American religious life is deeply entrenched and far-reaching, but it can be redressed in your church. Indeed the problem is complex; it is a participant, leadership, organizational, and spiritual issue. All the pieces must be addressed if we are to see greater commitment and participation in our churches.

Many of the reasons for the seeming decline of membership, involvement, and commitment to congregational life are quite complex. To truly understand and reverse what seems to be an inevitable pattern will require a spiritual revival and rethinking of how faith is lived and preached in contemporary society. But it will also require clergy and lay religious leaders to think multidimensionally—not only spiritually but also culturally, sociologically, and psychologically.

Is the lack of member involvement because the sheep no longer want to follow? In part, indeed it is. The social and cultural context in the United States has changed. Individualism and "what's in it for me?" consumerism have reshaped how Americans respond to commitment and relate to all institutions and organizations. Shepherds need to be aware of these changes and rework their leadership strategies to address the new context. However, congregational members also need to be shaped counterculturally through their involvement in the church. They need a vision for service and living out their faith personally and also in community in ways that challenge and invigorate them. The leadership of the church must find ways to shape the ministry and mission of the church so that attenders can contribute in ways that matter to them, in ways where they feel fulfilled and enlivened.

Do some Christians want a life of faith apart from the church? Yes, but usually it's because of disappointment with church as they know it. Oddly some want to remain affiliated with a church but at the same time stay disconnected from it. Faith develops through life in community and through ministry alongside others. We think that happens best through the organizational life of a healthily functioning church.

Is this "low bar" situation the fault of the shepherds? In part, indeed it is. The religious leader is called to lead the entire flock, not just those who follow effortlessly. Clergy need to acknowledge their role in this situation. In nearly all of the comments we heard or read from members, pastors figure prominently as both the problem and the solution. Church leaders need to recommit to the task of listening to the needs of all the members of the church and reshape the congregation to help sheep be more involved and raise participation levels. This can be addressed by rethinking membership and participation and the pastor's role in creating an engaged congregation.

Is the situation the result of an organizational problem? In part, indeed it is. While the parable suggests that responsibility lies with the shepherd alone, the problem is much more wide-reaching than clergy can tackle without help. It requires rethinking the activities of volunteering and committee work within the church. It necessitates the identification of the gifts and callings of all parts of the body: teaching such concepts as the priesthood of all believers, finding places for members to serve, giving them training, and recognizing their role in the mission of the church. It requires intentionality on the part of church leaders to be attentive and to track involvement, to structure accountability measures into how the church operates, to reach out to the marginalized, and to confront and if possible remedy the situations that led to separation.

Is it a spiritual problem? Yes, in part, indeed it is. For a long time many churches have tolerated a minimalist understanding of faith. Others have played down the implications of making a spiritual commitment to be a follower of Jesus Christ. Regrettably, it seems the spiritual bar has been set low over the decades—and centuries—more to add members than to create disciples. Yet there are very strong relationships across all our findings between those who say they are spiritually fulfilled and growing spiritually, and those who are highly committed and involved. To reinvigorate participation the church leadership must find ways to infuse ideas of service and volunteering with vision and purpose, mission and calling.

The most important question to emerge from this situation, the question that occupies much of the book, is what religious leaders can do to reach the less-committed persons associated with their congregations. In that regard we'll draw information from over one hundred thousand survey participants to show what motivates the most engaged attenders to contribute, and what causes the less-committed ones to become marginally involved. We'll also explore data from thousands of churches and hundreds of leaders to examine the practices that work or don't work in reengaging marginal members. We'll draw on what pastors in exemplary churches have done, and tap into the several quality books that uncover the best leadership practices for creating engagement. We'll report on commitment dynamics from some of the best and most representative surveys of America's churches, both the innovative and rapidly growing megachurches, which each author has studied intently, and other Protestant congregations of all sizes and traditions; as well as from several national studies of churches and churchgoers that we and others have conducted.

> Regrettably, it seems the spiritual bar has been set low over the decades—and centuries—more to add members than to create disciples.

All this comes with an important hope: we want to suggest very practical strategies that can stimulate a greater expression

of faith and increased involvement in the portion of God's kingdom that is the local church.

A Look at Reality

For most of the roughly three hundred thousand Protestant
churches in America only a small percentage of those in regular
attendance are active and engaged in mission and ministry. In
fact any church is highly unusual if more than half are. Nearly
all congregations bemoan this situation, but very few know how
to motivate greater participation.

Gallup surveys of Americans have shown that for decades
roughly 40 percent of Americans *say* they are in church weekly,
but recent actual counts of Christian attenders indicate that
perhaps no more than 22 percent of Protestants (and 25 percent of Catholics) actually show up in any given week. In fact
if the 40 percent (or 120 million of America's 300-plus million
population) who *said* they attend worship weekly did actually
arrive at the roughly three hundred thirty thousand Christian
congregations in the country, then each congregation would
average 360 in attendance. Yet currently the average attendance of America's Christian congregations is under 100. Likewise if 80 percent of the country claims Christianity as their
religion and 65 percent say they belong to a church, but only
about 40 percent show up sometime each month, then the
greatest American mission field may well already be the members of Christian churches.

Thus in most Christian flocks no more than half the "member" sheep are present. This situation is not isolated to any
one denomination. In general almost no national denomination draws more than half of its membership into worship services each week, as Table 1 illustrates. In a majority of U.S.
churches, regular attenders are often between 20 and 50 percent
of the congregation's overall membership. The attender-member
ratio also varies somewhat by the size of the congregation: the

Table 1 People join, but only half or less show up

Denominational Group, Year Reporting	Membership	Attendance	A/M Ratio
Nazarene Church, 2000	631,081	496,283	79%
Presbyterian Church, USA, 2006	2,266,808	1,058,607	47%
United Methodist Church, 2008	7,932,014	3,317,137	42%
Southern Baptist Convention, 2009	16,160,088	6,207,488	38%
Episcopal Church, 2006	2,154,572	765,326	36%
Evangelical Lutheran Church in America, 2009	4,542,868	1,289,953	28%

Table 2 The smaller the church, the more of its members who actually attend

Size of Congregation Based on All Persons Associated with It	Number of Churches, N = 2,409	Median Number of Regular Attenders, Including Children	Mean Percentage of All Associated Persons Who Are Weekly Attenders
7–49	302	20	58%
50–99	566	40	43%
100–249	785	75	40%
250–499	454	120	36%
500–999	188	200	34%
1,000–2,499	78	258	29%
2,500 and up	35	443	28%

Source: National Congregations Study, Protestant only (weighted).

smallest churches often have the highest proportion of members actually attending, as Table 2 shows.

However, only around 20 percent of the typical congregation both attends regularly and produces what might be described in sheep language as a full coat of wool, one that marks a person as a spiritually growing, engaged, and committed follower of Jesus Christ.

These tables are a snapshot of the present. Another motivation to give more attention to the group that's marginally connected to church is that it will probably keep increasing. Why? The biggest source of new church members is the *already converted*: waves of Christian immigrants into our country, births in our own families, or the circulation of saints from other congregations. That makes the number of totally unchurched nonbelievers in the country dramatically smaller than the inactive members in churches that we are calling the other 80 percent.

You might also think about your "missing" membership as a mission field. In doing so, we encourage you to aim at converting them into fully engaged participants, not merely volunteers or disconnected members. Don't give up on reaching out to new people, but turn serious attention to enriching the spiritual lives of those who call your church home. Explore how many marginal folks you have, who they are, and why they are disconnected—and not just in relation to a sacred Sunday moment but disconnected from the church community. Strive to enliven the spiritual experiences of longtimers throughout the week, deepening their faith commitments, challenging their knowledge of Scripture, training them in leadership, and calling out their gifts in service and in mission to others in ways that empower them rather than drain their willingness to be involved. Turn their culturally reinforced consumerism and their desire to customize their faith to meet their own spiritual needs into a commitment to live out the calling God has placed on their lives and the unique talents and purpose they have for personal ministry within the context of their church and the broader community.

Aim for Ongoing Maturity

Most churches work hard, sometimes very hard, at getting new people to come to church in the first place. But once they become members or regulars, is there an assumption that they will start finding their own way toward involvement and growth, and toward spiritual maturity? How much energy do you regularly put into creating a culture and programmatic reality that continue to develop long-term involvement and fulfillment? How can you keep challenging those who have been at the church ten, twenty, or even forty years to grow, mature, and remain faithful participants in the life of the church?

And what happens if they start to drift away at any point? Will you help those whose involvement has waned, especially those who have lowered their sights from loving God with all their heart, mind, soul, and strength? (Matthew 22:37–40).

In short, it's time to break the cycle of commitment mediocrity. This Introduction has already cited several biblical mandates. They include loving God, going after lost sheep, making disciples, and caring for the souls of your flock. Applying these teaching of Scripture will lead to a number of desirable results:

> It's time to break the cycle of commitment mediocrity.

1. You will offer spiritual care to a larger number of people already within the reach of your church's influence. These include those who once believed, and who may still believe, but who would also say they're not growing in their faith. One or more people in your church already have some level of relationship with these folks, and so you already have your foot (or toe) in the door to be a positive influence on them.

2. You will strengthen the witness of Christ to an unbelieving world. How many people do you know who say they believe in God but live as if they don't? As you help restore their walk with God and their fellowship with a church, you bring alignment to how outsiders view those who identify with Christ.

3. You will serve as a role model for others in breaking a long-entrenched pattern. How can so many congregations find

it acceptable to have so many absentee participants in their fold? Why are leaders willing to accept the popular mantra that only 20 percent of their congregation will do most of the work? What does it imply about the mission of the church that individuals think being a Christian and a "good church member" somehow authorizes them to attend infrequently and still claim faithfulness?

4. Your congregation's increased participation will be good for the health of your church itself. More spiritual care will happen as more people are involved in building up the body of Christ.

5. Your people's increased church involvement will also benefit the greater society. The more people who volunteer at church, the stronger our communities become, as Robert Putnam and others have documented so well (see the Bibliography).

We started this Introduction with a twist on one of Jesus' parables. The actual account (Matthew 18:10–14; Luke 15:1–7) implies what being a good shepherd entails. We are to leave the ninety-nine and search until we find the one lost sheep and return it to the fold. This ideal is so far from the norm in most churches today that most don't even aspire to it. We accept it as a sad reality and fail to aim anywhere near it. Or like the Apostle Paul, the things we know we should do, we don't, and those we try to avoid, we end up doing.

But things don't have to be this way—and for some they are not. If you are ready to explore further the challenge of turning more of your church's spectators into active disciples, please turn the page.

The Other 80 Percent

Part One

LISTENING

> If we could get more people to participate and share
> in the work to be done, we could do so much more.
> Those who joined in would get so much more out
> of their membership—spiritual growth, deeper/
> broader connections to other members, and that
> good feeling that you get when you know you are
> living the life God wants you to live.*

In almost every church a sizable group of members and attenders remain largely uninvolved. There is no single reason why this is so. Each less-than-active participant has unique grounds for his or her low level of involvement. As a result neither churches nor books addressing this situation can offer a one-size-fits-all solution to the problem of marginal participation. The best first step toward encouraging more active involvement is to listen to

---

*All quotations in this book are actual statements from people we interviewed or from written surveys we have used. Appendix B describes both processes. This epigraph comes from the parish inventories survey.

the reasons why some people are involved and why other people are not.

Your acts of listening will also help you draw in the allies needed to challenge the status quo. Virtually everyone, regardless of the level of participation, notices the dynamics of the situation; most feel it, and many lament it—even many of your less-involved contingents. However, your potential allies don't usually feel empowered to change the system. They need your courageous leadership to connect spiritually with those who are not plugged in.

The chapters in Part One will help you frame ways to *listen* to your congregation. Part Two will lay out the basis for what you need to *learn* about changing the system. Finally, Part Three will show you how best to *lead* all who identify with your church into a far more engaged level of committed involvement.

1

WHAT DO YOU HEAR
FROM THE COMMITTED
20 PERCENT?

Pat and Mary, a married couple in their late thirties who have one child, could be the poster children for their church of about one hundred people. They teach children's Sunday school weekly and love every minute of it. They are part of the welcome team on the second Sunday of each month, greeting people as they arrive, handing them a bulletin, and helping to pass the offering plates during the service. They each are on the rotation to read Scripture during worship. When training was offered to help people learn to be better Scripture readers, they were among the first to sign up. In fact they are present at all church activities, from potluck lunches to Saturdays of service in a low-income housing project near the church building.

They also invite relatives and friends to church, two of whom come regularly. They have big hearts for reaching out to others. Mary, who is more outgoing, often talks about her faith at work.

They also give 10 percent of their income through the church.

Pat and Mary affirm that they've experienced much spiritual growth during their time at the church. They had come to the church just after Mary became a Christian, influenced by a good friend who was attending the church at that time. Pat gladly came along and agrees that his faith has grown, especially as a men's group helped support and pray for him during two diffi- cult financial years when he changed jobs. As a couple they find great joy in helping their five-year-old son learn about Jesus. They appreciate all the ways their church provides spiritual nurturing for him, and for them as well.

We suspect most readers would want a church full of people like Pat and Mary—the kind of people who are highly involved and spiritually vibrant. Our statistics cannot discern if Pat and Mary or the other people described in this chapter are the best Christians, because our categories do not measure the amount of faith they have, their spiritual maturity, or their theological positions. Yet in terms of their involvement and relationship to the church, they are as close to the ideal as you will find.

If you listen carefully to the people described in this chapter, you will no doubt succeed in serving them well. It is important to learn who these "20 percent" are and why they are connecting at your church.

You will find two groups of people in this chapter. Each group has something different to teach you. The good news is that these two groups are the easiest to hear from.

One group is the *already* committed—those with the highest participation levels. They tend to be your core people. They are engaged with spirit, emotion, and energy. By all indications in the research, they are growing spiritually as well.

The other group is represented by people moving *toward* greater commitment. This group has become increasingly involved in church over the past few years. They are excited, energized, and are also experiencing spiritual growth.

By comparison, understanding the dynamics of your less-active participants and absentee members is a considerably more difficult task.

Even though your less-active members typically outnumber your committed people, they are much less frequently heard from. (Of course there are the occasional squeaky-wheel members, who endlessly inform church leaders about the problems, disappointments, and perceived dysfunction they see in the congregation.) However, most of these members are rarely even seen, whether in worship, at church functions or groups, or in the church office. With such limited communication, how can you come to know more about them and their needs? How can you discover why these members have drifted away, and more importantly, what should you do to reengage them in an active faith within the church community?

We heard from people at all levels of participation thanks to three large datasets, which we shorthandedly refer to as "congregational life," "parish profiles," and "larger churches" surveys. (Each dataset is described in detail in Appendix B.) Together they represent over one hundred thousand Protestant churchgoers in the United States. We created a scale of factors to measure members' level of participation in the life of the congregation. This scale included their worship attendance level, involvement in small groups, committees and service programs, level of giving, level of inviting others, and number of close friends at the church. From there we compared profiles of each level of participation from highest to lowest. We also examined the groups of members who said they had either increased or decreased their level of involvement over the past two years. From this analysis we constructed an involvement continuum (see Table 1.1) and explored how these groups differed from each other on a host of spiritual and attitudinal questions.

Table 1.1 Everyone is somewhere on a continuum of involvement

Participation Level	Characteristics
High involvement	Attend, give, invite, serve, lead, develop deep friendships
Medium involvement	Attend less frequently, might give, have friendships
Low involvement, nonattenders, dropouts	Attend rarely or never yet have some affiliation past or present, might still give, might have friendships

This chapter listens to those who are on the more involved side, the roughly 20 percent who seem to do most of the work of the church. The next chapter will attend to the voices of the less involved, those we are calling the other 80 percent.

Those Who Are Already Committed

Your most involved members and participants are just that—involved. Not surprisingly, people who are involved give more, attend church frequently, invite other people to church, participate in committees and groups, have more close friends at the church, and have been at the church longer than less-involved folks.

There is a good chance that you already know and listen to these "good sheep" in your congregation. They may include most of your leadership team, such as elders, deacons, and volunteers in Sunday school and infant nursery. They are the active participants that the entire congregation relies on week after week.

It is relatively easy to listen to these folks and to find out what they are thinking or feeling about the state of their church or their personal spiritual development. They are present and active in the life of the church. That means they're easily accessible, and they're often comfortable in joining constructive discussions about the church. All a pastor needs to do is make the time to inquire and then trust that they will provide honest feedback.

They Love Their Church Most

This choice group, as represented in our data, is more likely to be older. They are also more likely to be married. Not surprisingly they are also more frequently the longer-term members at the church. Some lament the fact that certain people keep doing everything. As one woman said, "In running [the church], it's always the same people just changing jobs." Others love what they do and want to spread that joy:

> If we could get more people to participate and share in the work to be done, we could do so much more and those who joined in would get so much more out of their membership—spiritual growth, deeper/broader connections to other members, and that good feeling that you get when you know you are living the life God wants you to live.

High-participation people are also more likely to see the church as having a clear vision, goals, and purpose, and they are strongly committed to it. Additionally these folks have a very strong and clear sense of the church's identity and how it differs from other churches. Not only do they know what the church stands for, but they are more likely to find it easy to tell others what is unique about the church. Above all, they are personally comfortable with this identity.

Likewise they have a very optimistic picture of the congregation. They perceive the church's overall morale as higher than do less-involved persons. They also more strongly agree that there is a sense of excitement about the church's future. Additionally, more than other participants, they perceive the congregation as ready to try new things.

In relation to the congregational community they are more inclined to perceive the members as very highly likely to help one another in times of trouble. They also affirm more strongly than other participants that factors like their friends, the adult education, and the social outreach keep them at the church.

But with this rosy picture you may be surprised to learn they don't always agree that church members are well informed about what committees and groups are doing. Further, they are less likely to think that adequate study is regularly undertaken for church planning, or that the neighboring community is aware of the church's programs. They also feel that the theological and biblical implications of decisions should be discussed more openly, and that disagreements should be dealt with honestly and openly.

Essentially they are a bit more concerned than members of other involvement groups about the communications and functioning of the church. In part this is perhaps because they have invested the most, cared the most, and felt the most positive toward the church. Out of their commitment to the church comes a somewhat more critical concern for how well it functions. Likewise, because of their increased involvement in leadership they are probably more likely to see and experience the deficiencies of the organization more pointedly.

Contrary to common assumptions, this group is no more likely than others to be satisfied with elements of the Sunday worship, such as its style of music. Nor do they rate the pastor or the denominational identity more highly than other members do as factors that keep them coming back to their church.

But they are much more likely to affirm that the church's worship services and its activities do help them with everyday living. Highly involved people also stand out in their strong emphasis that the church encourages them to serve the wider world. And they demonstrate this by being the most likely group to volunteer time in social service outside the church.

> Highly involved people also stand out in their strong emphasis that the church encourages them to serve the wider world.

This group really stands out in the area of spiritual growth and fulfillment. There are huge differences here compared to the less involved (see Table 1.2). The most highly involved members are much more likely to affirm that being at the church has made a difference in their spiritual life. These highest-level participants are also much more likely to agree that their spiritual needs are being met. They strongly affirm that they have had much growth in the faith in the past year.

Table 1.2 The most involved rate their churches much higher in certain areas

	Low Participation	Medium Participation	High Participation
Strong sense of belonging	27%	49%	67%
Church helps me find and use my gifts to a great extent	18%	34%	53%
Strongly agree that my spiritual needs are being met	22%	38%	54%
Have a strong sense of excitement about church's future	20%	31%	48%
My faith grew much in the past year due to the church	19%	36%	54%

Source: U.S. Congregational Life Survey, 2008/09.

Highly involved members also feel strongly that they are being encouraged by the church leadership to discover their gifts for ministry and to use them to get involved. And they are the most likely group to assert that they have a strong sense of belonging at the church, even after statistically controlling for the influence of their length of time at the church and other factors known to increase a sense of belonging.

Theologically they are more "orthodox" in their beliefs about the Bible and more likely to affirm Jesus as the only way to salvation, Jesus' literal resurrection from the dead, and the view that the Bible has the answers for daily living. Additionally, more than other groups they like sermons that are biblically based and illustrated. They also score higher on frequency of personal daily devotions.

Listening to Why They Are Engaged

None of these findings will come as a great surprise to the astute pastor or church leader. After all, this highly engaged group is the one clergy have the most exposure to. However, it is instructive to think about this group from the perspective of why and how they have become so involved. What exactly is it that they love about their church and its leaders that motivates them to be so engaged?

Worship trappings don't necessarily connect them and keep them highly involved, according to our analysis. Likewise it isn't merely that they have good friends at church. Rather, this group is involved in the life of the church on many levels. Together the multiple involvements contribute to these members' sense of spiritual satisfaction and personal enrichment.

As we will continue to suggest throughout the book, *you can and should continue to strengthen those connections and involvements that increase participation, and make congregational life even more spiritually meaningful for your most committed participants.*

The following comments from several highly involved people suggest ways they became engaged and yet also long for further connections.

> My hope is that while I grow in my personal faith, I am able to contribute my gifts and talents in order to make my church better for my church family and for visitors.

> It is very rare that you join a church that has a lot of opportunities for ministry. You know there's a lot more ministry opportunities here than at the church where I came from, so that made the difference [for me in getting involved].

> I wish that I had the same involvement that I did while being confirmed.

You don't want to exhaust or burn out these stellar members. Nor do you want them to stagnate such that they feel underappreciated, unengaged, or spiritually unfulfilled. Without challenges or adequate personal rewards, such as helping them train to be better leaders or increasing their sense of responsibility or acknowledging a job well done, they may detour into the feeling that all they're doing is church busywork.

Those Currently Increasing Their Involvement

Another important group to identify and listen to are those who would say their involvement has increased in the past two years. In fact in many ways they are more important to listen to than those who have been heavily engaged for a long time. Those who are already committed can tell you what you did right in the past. Those who are becoming increasingly engaged can help you know what you are currently doing to facilitate their involvement and growth.

Unfortunately this group of people who are increasing their involvement is not always evident to a church's leadership team. You cannot spot them just by sight. It's not like they wear a button or T-shirt that reads, "I have recently increased my level of involvement."

However, you can find them in your own church by observation and asking around. Or you can identify them as we did by surveying your congregation and including a question like, "How has your participation in this church's activities *changed* in the last two years?" (The response options we used were (1) increased, (2) remained the same, (3) decreased, and (4) I haven't been here two years.) You can also invite them to self-select: "Later this month we want to offer some training to people who have become more involved in recent months. If you have accepted a new responsibility, we'd like to honor you, give you some orientation, and offer you some very practical help."

Similarities and Differences with the Highly Involved

In most cases those who have recently increased their involvement are potentially "best participants" in the making. Their activity level is quite similar to those who are highly committed.

Figure 1.1 The longer people have been at a church, the less they say their participation is increasing

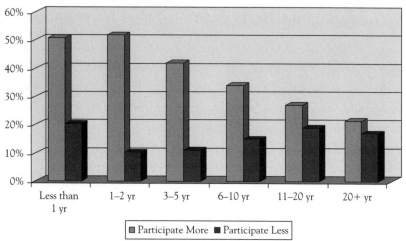

Participation Change During Last Two Years by Time at Church

■ Participate More   ■ Participate Less

Source: U.S. Congregational Life Survey, 2008/09.

They attend worship, give generously, have a number of good friends at the church, and are increasingly involved in groups and committees, and in service programs.

Yet their demographic patterns are quite different from the picture painted of the most highly involved. These increasingly involved participants have been coming to the church for less time (Figure 1.1) and are more likely to be younger (Figure 1.2). Distance from the church doesn't make a difference unless they live more than a thirty-minute drive from the church, and then they are less likely to increase participation.

For this group, family household configuration also shows distinct differences from the highly participatory group and from the remaining congregation. Couples without children are less likely to have increased their participation, while adults with children are more likely. Married attenders are neither more nor less likely, but people who are single, in committed relationships, or divorced are more likely to have increased their

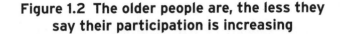

Figure 1.2 The older people are, the less they say their participation is increasing

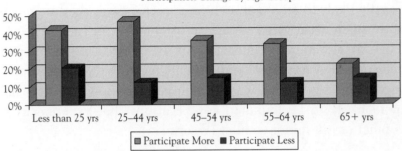

Source: U.S. Congregational Life Survey, 2008/09.

participation in the past two years, while widowed attenders are less likely. No significant differences related to income, education, employment status, or occupation distinctly characterizes this group from other groups.

This group portrays a distinctive and telling interaction with church dynamics that seems to relate to their reasons for increased involvement. These more-participating people score higher in saying their church encourages them to find and use their gifts than those whose involvement is unchanged or in decline. They indicate that the church has made an effort to get them involved and has provided opportunities for leadership. They also see the leadership as more willing to try new things, and they strongly affirm that the pastor takes into account the ideas of those who worship at the church.

These persons are also more likely to say that the church and its members are of great help in times of trouble than those in the congregation whose participation is unchanged or in decline. Somewhat surprising, while the number of close friends in the church is positively related to increased participation, it is not as strongly correlated to a rise in involvement as many of the other dynamics.

The increasingly involved members also sense that worship services are more likely to help them with their everyday lives. Predictably these folks invite more people, and while they are equally likely to attend church on a weekly basis, they are much more likely than other groups to attend several times a week. They are also more optimistic about the church's future and perceive a higher morale within the congregation. Not too surprising, people who are increasing their participation are somewhat more likely to be found in congregations that experience no conflict or just minor conflict (Figure 1.3).

Spiritual Issues Are Very Important

Most dramatically the data on this group show an overwhelmingly strong correlation between this increased participation and having a rich, strengthening "spiritual life." All the surveys we used left the definition of "a satisfying, fulfilling spiritual life" up

**Figure 1.3 The less conflict, the higher
the level of participation**

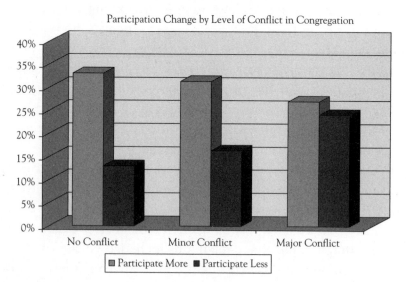

Source: U.S. Congregational Life Survey, 2008/09.

to the respondents—what they perceived it to be for themselves. Likewise this group strongly affirms that their spiritual needs are being met and that they are satisfied with worship. They report greater levels of spiritual growth and attribute it directly to the church's efforts rather than external sources or their own independent spiritual pursuits. They also have a very strong sense of belonging to the congregation. This perception exists even though these persons have been at the church less time and are generally younger than the full population, with large numbers coming from traditionally more marginalized groups in church life, such as singles and the divorced.

There is clearly a strong spiritual component to increased participation, but other dimensions of the church and personal conditions also play in increased participation. This can be best seen in the reasons these persons select for why their participation has increased (six response options were offered, and respondents could choose more than one). Table 1.3 shows the percentage of the 7,299 people in the parish inventory survey who said their participation had increased because of these reasons.

The table affirms that participation increased when a number of components were present. There needed to be *opportunity* for involvement (office or new responsibility), *motivation* for increased participation (stronger faith and, for some, children), and the *ability* to be more involved (time and better

Table 1.3 Increased participation results mostly from a new role or responsibility

Reason Given for Increased Participation in Last Two Years	Percentage
Accepted office or other new responsibility in the church	57
Health had improved	28
Due to their children	15
Had a more positive attitude toward the church	4

Source: Parish inventory survey.

health). Across the datasets we used, the responses of those who had increased their involvement confirmed this three-part combination. These people perceived the church to be making efforts to provide them with opportunities by electing them, appointing them, or asking them to serve. They received training to discover and develop their gifts, and support to try new things. Their motive for increased participation is in part perhaps the satisfaction of being "called" into greater service and ministry, using their talents for God, or simply as mundane as being recognized and asked to help. But at its root much of this motivation is interpreted as or equated with a spiritual catalyst.

Clinton, one of the people we interviewed, models the way these factors can come together for participation to increase. Clinton is in a second marriage and in his forties. He and his family had been active in a small church for many years, but it went through what he calls a "nasty split." As his family relocated to their present church four years ago, Clinton had one goal, and not a very spiritual one at that, he admits: "I came here to hide," he says. "I was kind of a wounded veteran." But it didn't work for him. As hard as he tried to lay back and do nothing, week after week during the worship service he was "so stirred [that] I couldn't sit in my seat another moment—and I really tried." As he explains, "I looked at the bulletin and . . . I just could feel something inside of me beginning to burn that says, 'I want you to get involved in that.' It moved me and moved me. Even as much as I tried to ignore it for six months and I couldn't ignore it any longer, [so] I went and volunteered. . . . It was the Holy Spirit just drawing me."

From then on, Clinton has taken on an increasing amount of responsibility. Today he's a prayer team captain, a member of the church's vision board, a member of a care team, and a small-group leader.

Just as Clinton sees his involvement through a lens of spiritual motivation and spiritual development, so do others.

They consistently include a spiritual factor in their expressed desires that others too will move toward greater involvement. These quotes attest to this impulse while they also hint at the ways churches could promote this growth:

> We need more emphasis on [the] spiritual growth of individuals and helping them find their place in ministry. This will help draw the people who participate on the fringe into the center of our church community.

> I want to see the congregation get good at being church. The more clearly it communicates its vision for how this church makes disciples of Jesus, the more it will succeed.

> I would like to see more development of lay leadership and more emphasis on spiritual growth of individual members. I think many hidden talents in the area of leading worship are left untouched.

> I would hope for the church's reinvigoration and energy so people can attend church, seek spiritual refreshment, guidance, and fellowship without the weight of being a part of a small army of individuals who have to tend to the day-to-day matters of the church. People following their passion in their church involvement will turn this church around.

The point we draw from quotes like these and the survey data is that for those who increase their participation, their sense of spiritual fulfillment directly correlates with greater involvement in the congregation. The idea of spiritual fulfillment is individually defined. We don't always know what each person means by the term. We just know that they link two things together: greater involvement helps their sense of spiritual growth. Likewise a sense of spiritual growth increases participation. On the basis of our research it is absolutely clear that these two are intertwined.

> Their sense of spiritual fulfillment directly correlates with greater involvement in the congregation.

What is less clear is which comes first: the increased involvement, or the increased sense of spiritual fulfillment and spiritual needs being met. Our "larger church survey" hints at an answer. In it we asked people about the primary path in their move from spectator to participant. The path most likely to lead to increased participation was the spiritual motivation path ("I responded to an inward sense of call or spiritual prompting"). Other options, such as bulletin announcements, invitations from people they knew, and invitations from people they did not know, were unrelated to their increased involvement.

Certainly increased participation happens through a combination of effects working together. Clinton talked about seeing service opportunities in the bulletin. But he also spoke about things stirring and burning inside of him that he attributed to the tug of the Holy Spirit. Our guess is that on the survey, where he was limited to one choice, he would have checked the spiritual motivation option: "I responded to an inward sense of call or spiritual prompting."

Help Them Take Their Next Step

One of the surveys we used for this book listed sixteen items and asked participants which they'd like to see their church strengthen in order to help them increase their involvement (see Table 1.4). The most important thing to learn is that there is a great diversity of opinion among the twenty-five thousand persons who responded. None of the sixteen items received more than 12 percent. Yet each response option got some responses.

The implication? People attend church for different reasons and want different things from their experience. Likewise strengthening one aspect of the church may increase the

**Table 1.4 Most churches need multiple pathways
to help increase involvement**

For the sake of your own personal involvement in your congregation, which one task would you most like to see strengthened?	*Percentage*
Helping members deepen their personal and spiritual relationship with God	12
Helping members discover their own gifts for ministry and service	10
Providing Christian education for children and youth	8
Offering worship that provides a meaningful experience of God and the Christian tradition	8
Helping members understand their use of time, talents, and money as expressions of Christian stewardship	7
Encouraging members to act on the relationship of the Christian faith to social, political, and economic issues	6
Providing fellowship opportunities for members	6
Providing a caring ministry for the sick, shut-ins, and the bereaved	6
Participating in activities and programs with other local religious groups	5
Expressing our denominational heritage/tradition	5
Providing worship that expresses the Gospel in contemporary language and forms	5
Providing Christian education programs for adults	5
Sharing the good news of the Gospel with the unchurched	5
Engaging in acts of charity and service for persons in need	5
Providing pastoral counseling to help members deal with personal problems	5
Supporting the global mission of the church	2

Source: Hartford Institute parish inventory.

involvement of a small percentage of attenders, but to engage many folks the church has to approach the matter differently. We think the key is not in a specific menu of choices so much as in helping people do more of whatever has been fostering their spiritual fulfillment at the church to date. If you can help them identify and take a next step, then we suspect they will report that they are continuing to grow.

Remember Groups in Transition

Every church can identify specialized patterns of church involvement—variations over time stemming from challenges in life situations, such as college, a new baby, illness, retirement, and aging. This is especially important for congregations full of retirees and aging baby boomers. Active-participation norms and values will have to be reconceptualized and reformulated to make the most of these key participants so as to keep them vital and involved with a true sense of engagement.

One example is a church that provides a Mom's Day Out program for new mothers. Another church does seasonal work with students from nearby universities, training them in leadership and campus evangelism. Another church in a university corridor offers programs for visiting scholars. A Florida church accommodates "snowbirds," doing meet-the-church welcome events and opening ways for them to do partial-year ministry.

Drawing Them In and Keeping Them

Hopefully you felt encouraged as you read this chapter. Maybe you had not realized that you have two kinds of active folks: those who are already committed, and those who are increasing their involvement. Perhaps it has been helpful to imagine specific aspects of your church that have drawn those with high or increasing levels of commitment. We trust you found it reassuring that people make a connection between their participation and their spiritual growth.

We now want to build on this chapter in three ways:

1. We certainly encourage you to keep listening to those who are committed. Let them tell you what you did that

was right. Listen to those who are moving toward greater involvement as they tell you what you are doing well. Learn who they are and why they're increasingly connected.

2. It is equally important to understand those with declining and minimal participation. If a church's leadership is attuned only to listen and respond to the voices of the most involved participants, the others are left to sit on the sidelines, attending only infrequently, participating marginally, or never connecting except at holidays, weddings, baptisms, and funerals. Chapter Two will profile these people.

3. The dynamics that draw people in and integrate them into a church are typically different from those that keep them there. That is why so many churches see a huge loss of people out the back door and why, in particular, participation can begin to decline within two years. Chapter Three will teach you how to create a listening team, not only for your committed and involved people but also for others whom you may not be hearing.

If you keep the model you have now, you'll get the 20 percent—those who are highly involved. If you augment your participation model based on that group, that's who you will get. But you will probably need a diversified model to reach all the other groups in your church. Each participation group tells you something different about the congregation's needs, how to lead them to be more in volved, and ultimately how to help them develop and grow spiritually. Our goal is to help you pastor your entire flock, including the other 80 percent.

2

WHAT DO YOU HEAR
FROM THE LESS-COMMITTED
80 PERCENT?

Our Sunday worship services need more life, joy,
[and] challenge. Sunday worship used to be a must
for me, a time I would not miss because it spiritually
filled me and set my week off. We don't have that
spirit anymore. I attend more out of "obligation"
than "I wouldn't miss it," and I don't attend near as
much anymore.

It is somewhat painful for us, even as researchers, to listen to the
voices of the less connected. The spiritual despair and sense of
religious meaninglessness in their comments is a powerful por-
trayal of their fragile relationship to their churches.

We imagine it is even more difficult for pastors and other
church leaders to hear these persons. Perhaps some readers
would dismiss the comments in this chapter with the rationale,
"Thankfully, the person you just quoted does not reflect the attitudes of *my* church members." But are you sure? Might these
comments and attitudes also reside in the large percentage of
members who seldom attend and even less often participate in
the life of your church? And how would you know unless you
intentionally made the effort to listen to them?

Before you launch into such an effort in your church, first
get a sense of the patterns that emerged from roughly thirteen
thousand persons across several surveys. We'll start with those
who said their involvement decreased in the past two years.

Then we'll hear from those with the lowest level of participation. Finally we'll listen to those who almost never attend and to full dropouts.

Those with Declining Involvement

Predictably the profile of people whose participation has decreased in recent years looks like the direct opposite of those in the previous chapter. Folks with decreasing involvement (on average they constitute 10–20 percent of a congregation) are likely to be cycling off committees, heading to college, changing jobs, dealing with illnesses, or having family difficulties. Often we assume that many of them are disconnecting because they are unhappy with the pastor or other members. Or maybe they are disgruntled about worship decisions, new directions in mission efforts, or how the money is being spent.

Our data in part confirm all these factors as being related to less involvement. However, much of what underlies the conditions and circumstances for decreased involvement seems to have more to do with *spiritual* issues than it does with circumstantial and experiential issues. This finding about the importance of spiritual factors is similar to what those with increased involvement expressed in the previous chapter. The parish inventory study specifically asked the reasons for decline in involvement. Table 2.1 presents those figures.

Less-involved people are marked by a lack of motivation: their faith and commitment to the church are in decline. Their opportunities have diminished: they no longer have a place to serve nor as much time to do it. And surprisingly a small percentage are less able to be involved in the church because of health and child-rearing issues.

These findings challenge a few of our cherished assumptions about a lack of involvement. Stereotypes of animosity toward the church, issues with children, and health-related difficulties seem less influential than we often tend to think.

Table 2.1 Participation decreases as motive, means, and ability disappear

Reason Given for Decreased Participation in Last Two Years	Percentage
Faith had gotten weaker	34
Had less time	34
Ended office or position service	27
Had a more negative view of the church	25
Due to their children	10
Health had declined	5

Source: Parish Inventory Survey. Respondents could choose more than one reason, so the percentages will not total 100.

As we looked more closely at the information from those who said their participation was in decline, we found a pattern similar to Willow Creek's Reveal effort (see Appendix B). In many congregations across these different studies, participation decreased the longer a person was a member at the church and the older an attender was.

Certainly we can't keep increasing our involvement the longer we are at church because there comes a point where it's impossible to be even more involved. This reality is compounded as a person grows older.

Yet that's not the concern here. The data show that these patterns of decreasing involvement exhibit themselves far before having been many years at the church or the onset of old age (recall Figures 1.1 and 1.2). Surprisingly within two years of being at church, a decline in participation intensity is evident. Apparently churches are much better at creating initial commitment than they are at sustaining and enhancing that involvement. This reality is compounded by the fact that many churches have programs for new people, but very few have them for those continuing to develop a life of faith. Many congregations have done away with adult education or diminished it in favor of having more people at worship services.

> Churches are much better at creating initial commitment than they are at sustaining and enhancing that involvement.

If we remove the influence of age and time at the church, then the only personal factor that seems to be influential in contributing to decreasing one's involvement is how unsettled one's family or personal life is. Perhaps a person is undergoing stress, might be moving soon, or has become ill. No other *personal* characteristic, such as education level, income, employment status, occupation, family household configuration, marital status, or having children seemed to greatly decrease involvement generally across the surveys.

By contrast a whole set of internal *congregational* factors did greatly contribute to diminished involvement. As one person wrote in a parish profile:

> I realized that I could not describe what makes our church unique, what it stands for. I do not have close friends in the church at this time and I think that all makes a big difference in my regular attendance, regardless of time, distance and health.

Such persons had a vague and indefinite sense of what the church stands for. They also indicated a weaker perception of their church's vision. Additionally this group was less likely to claim that the church had a clear vision and purpose. Compared then to others, they were less likely to know what the church's vision might be, that their congregation was unique, or that they could adequately express what it stood for to others. It is impossible to know whether this perception was the cause of their decreased participation or a result. However, one thing is certain: their understanding of the church's vision will not be strengthened by their lack of attendance and involvement.

This process of disconnection becomes a slippery slope that will lead them out of the church.

What is more, this group of people with decreasing participation felt a lack of attention from church leadership. Those who said their participation decreased were more likely to note that the church had not done a good job of helping them find their gifts and use them. Nor did they feel adequately trained, compared to others. These persons also perceived the church's leadership to be making fewer efforts to get them involved. They reported lower evaluations of their churches in terms of equal opportunities for leadership positions and being open to trying new things, again compared to more-involved members of the same churches. Here is an example from the parish profiles:

> I am less involved of late because I never really found a place to really fit in to render services. We need more seminars and classes for adults. The church needs to use the services of all members and not just a few. A lot of the members are getting lost in the church and are not being recognized for what they contribute.

They were more likely to say that the pastor didn't take into account the ideas of those who worship there—meaning themselves—and that church leadership was less supportive of the programs they needed and wanted. Here are two examples, again from the parish profiles, exactly as they were written:

> Although I was an EXTREMELY active member about 5 years ago, my enthusiasm for our church has definitely waned and I now attend only once or twice a month. I believe we have lost our focus on missions. I have begun attending other churches in which their focus is more mission-oriented.

> It may just be my impression, but I have stopped volunteering because I have been turned off by the attitude and lack of attention given to children's worship and education.

Not too surprising, this group had an overall pessimistic appraisal of their congregation's morale. They were unlikely to identify a sense of excitement about the future at their church. They also felt the congregation was less helpful to them in times of trouble. But interestingly their diminished involvement was only slightly related to having fewer friends at the church.

> I've struggled the most with the "What keeps you here?" question. Truthfully, I'm not sure what keeps me here. I have some friends here, but even if I attended another church I know we would still keep in touch. I think I stay here because it's status quo for right now. But I am not sure that I will continue to stay. I've lost my sense of belonging here.

One might assume that for all attenders, the longer someone has been at the church, the stronger the sense of belonging will be. However, taking into account the previous quote and the group's survey patterns, this seems not to be the case for everyone in the congregation. The congregational and leadership factors that most correspond to the gradual disconnection of these members promote a weaker sense of belonging even though their longer time at the church, their age, and friendships should be strengthening this commitment.

> I joined here ten plus years ago because of a spiritual pastor and many friends but at present am looking for another church where I can be spiritually fed and energized. Good friends are not enough to sustain me. A church should be more than that. Presently our church is more like a club.

Material from surveys, comments, and interviews suggests that the move to lessened involvement is a gradual drift toward detachment. This includes a multitude of individualized reasons as precipitating factors for disconnection. Some reasons speak of things lacking, such as excitement, age-specific groups, or training. Some complain of cliques. Some seem unavoidable, like illness and aging. Some perhaps didn't have to be, such as conflict within the church. Some deal with changes in the church resulting in unhappiness with worship, or dissatisfaction with the pastor, or disagreement with a theological shift.

Ultimately most in this group describe their disconnection from church in spiritual terms. This decline in participation is tied statistically most strongly to a diminished sense of spiritual growth and a stronger perception that spiritual needs are not being met.

Overall this group is perhaps the most negative spiritually, regarding the church as a whole. They are less spiritually fulfilled than others except some of those who never attend. What prominently underlies a decline in involvement is a lack of spiritual fulfillment and spiritual satisfaction.

In reality this body of people is perhaps the most crucial group for church leaders to listen to. They have the most to share with church leadership about what isn't working. They are the red flags, the warning signs, the emergency alarms in a congregation. Unfortunately in most cases they are not obvious or even noticeable. Rather, these persons often just drift away, quietly slipping into the margins of congregational life, intent on not drawing attention to themselves. In many cases we heard them blaming themselves for their reduction in involvement and their sense of being less spiritually fulfilled, when in fact the church programs and leadership were also to blame. Here is how one person phrased it:

> **This body of people is perhaps the most crucial group for church leaders to listen to.**

I long for personal, meaningful, deeply spiritual, and social connections with other people in my stage of life at church. I want that smaller sense of community within my church family. I would love to have a close-knit circle of friends at church the way my parents' generation does. I would love for us to be the kind of church that people want to come participate in and be a part of. I don't know the answer of how to make it happen at my church. . . . Much of it is probably my fault, but I just don't feel spiritually connected here.

Those with Low or Marginal Involvement

If it is difficult for church leadership to perceive those who are slowly shuffling to the sidelines, it is quite easy to identify another major group. One reason is that they are often as much as a third of the total membership. This group has the lowest level of participation. These folks may attend, but they do little else; they are literally spectators. They are seldom a focus of study, perhaps because church leaders think they already know all about them—they do nothing but sit, right? However, a close look at this group reveals at least four distinct subgroups with different needs and patterns of relationship with the church.

Guests and Newcomers

This first low or marginal subgroup is the easiest to isolate. Most churches have a distinct population of people who are either brand-new or still visiting the church. These folks don't exactly qualify as members but rather as persons yet to be drawn into the congregation. They could be categorized as marginal attenders.

Although they are very important, they are a bit outside the scope of this book. Your church should have a hospitality, guest relations, or first-timers team to deal specifically with this group. Many good books exist to help newcomers move toward participation, involvement, and spiritual growth. Some recommended titles include Gary McIntosh, *Beyond the First Visit: The Complete Guide to Connecting Guests at Your Church* (Baker, 2006); Larry Osborne, *Sticky*

Church (Zondervan, 2008); and Mark Waltz, *Lasting Impressions: From Visiting to Belonging* (Group, 2008).

Dating but Undecided

The second subgroup of marginal attenders has been there longer than a newcomer. You might consider these folks as dating, with marriage or engagement a definite uncertainty. This group is likely to include newer people, attenders who are not members, and those (especially in the case of the megachurch attenders) who divide their loyalties and attendance between several "church homes."

In addition to their very low levels of participation, these folks have a perception of the church that's considerably distinct from any other group in the congregation. They have an essentially positive perception of the church; thus they come and attend. But they are not well aware of the goals, direction, or vision of the church. They don't feel strongly (either positively or negatively) about the church leadership or its organizational structures, because they don't know about them. They are often significantly more liberal in their theological beliefs and less engaged in personal spiritual practices. They have fewer friends at church and are less comfortable with the church's identity, but they are not uncomfortable with it.

Some in this group seem to attend the church because of their children. They come to give their children religious education rather than for their own spiritual edification, so they keep the church at arm's distance. Compared to the involved members, people in this group are not likely to have found or used their gifts. They are more likely to have a lower sense of church morale, less sense of excitement, and less feeling of belonging. This is mostly due to the fact that a large percentage of this group "don't know" or are "unsure" about the church.

Their indifference does not indicate that they are significantly more negative, therefore uninvolved. They are not angry or full of animosity, but rather are neutral and in essence dis-connected. They are on the bench, watching and waiting to be put into the game. They haven't yet been engaged or inspired to participate more fully. They are the church's field, ripe for harvest. They are potentially active participants if the church's leadership can find ways to engage them.

One person we talked with exactly fit this model. George was in his midthirties and recently divorced. The divorce caused him to move to a different town, and he was looking for places to connect with other people. He hadn't been to church since his childhood but was attracted to First Church because of its location in the center of a quaint New England town just two blocks from his home.

He attended off and on, once or twice a month, for nearly a year. During that time he received handshakes, polite conver-sation, and what he interpreted as mildly flirty behavior from the three single females in the congregation. He also received literature about the church in the mail. He liked what he heard the pastor say from the pulpit and also the social outreach efforts.

Yet no one had asked him to help. Nor did he feel that any-one had encouraged him to be involved. He never thought of joining and didn't see inserting himself in the church's affairs, because he couldn't see how he could help them. Following the divorce, he wasn't sure if anyone wanted him. The church's lack of personal outreach to the marginal participants in the sanctu-ary seemed to reinforce this feeling.

Over and again in our surveys we received comments about the lack of member outreach and its contribution to keep-ing this group sitting on the sideline, uninvolved. If you listen closely to the least-involved attenders, you can hear the longing for involvement and suggestions for methods of reconnection. Here's an example:

> I attended another local church for 18 years and loved it and was very involved in the women's ministries and children programs.

We switched churches because my son likes it here and we live closer to this church. I have not found the church very friendly though. We have attended services weekly for three years and the only people we know are people we already knew from activities outside the church. We have never been asked or invited to be part of any activity other than through newsletters and sign-up sheets. And the church wonders why so few people actively participate!

Connected and Needy but Uncommitted

A third subgroup of highly marginal members has its own distinctive pattern of interaction with the church. This group is composed of those who attend worship services very infrequently (less than once a month). Compared to others at the lowest end of our participation scale, these infrequent attenders have been at the church a long time, with as many as a third having attended over twenty years. Many of them have friends at the church, give money to the church, and may even be part of a group or ministry. However, they almost never show up.

Members of this group stand out when they do show up. They know people. Everyone greets them as if they were long-lost relatives, perhaps even prodigal sons. Some even jokingly make a big deal of them finally showing up for church. Such greetings are often uncomfortable, and they highlight the reality that these folks seldom participate. It isn't surprising that this group most often attends at holy days, when the church is full of similar people. It is less likely that any of them will be singled out as "deficient" participants if the church is full of such people. Church leaders teach their hospitality teams how to greet newcomers, but how often are greeters instructed in ways to welcome with sensitivity the prodigal participant?

While some of these less-involved members have drifted away because of a lack of interest or lack of spiritual satisfaction, the surveys and individual comments suggest that other reasons

might also contribute to this pattern. Without careful listening and sensitive follow-up, however, the underlying issues may
never be addressed by church leadership. This group has significantly more youth, singles, and divorced or separated persons—
in other words fewer married couples. If the norms of the church
favor married couples, with or without children, persons in other
family configurations may feel excluded. As one woman said,
"Just recently I strayed away [from attending]. . . . I'm a single
parent with [few places to fit in]."

This group was also filled with persons in need of help of
all sorts. Comments on the surveys suggested that life circumstances and family changes play a significant role in this group's
lack of attendance. The vast majority of these traumatic situations could easily be addressed by the church leadership, and
support could be provided.

But listen also to the sense of guilt and embarrassment at
play in the feelings of not measuring up to a perfectionist attitude these people perceive in their congregations. Likewise
many of these persons express a lack of outreach, pastoral care,
and just plain compassion from their church.

> I had gone through a bankruptcy and lost my home and just, I
> [was] kind of depressed and . . . and I know that God was with
> me but still wanted to stay away from a crowd you know.

> I was going through things with my son and I just kind of drifted
> away. And the biggest thing for me was I wasn't able to pay my
> pledge and that really bothered me. So once the finances got
> short, I guess I felt bad not being able to contribute, you know.
> And then that led to not coming. And no one from the church
> ever came to ask why I wasn't around.

> Over the past year my schedule has become increasingly hectic
> [causing] me to miss many, many Sundays—sometimes going
> 6 weeks or more without attending church after nearly 4 years

of attending regularly. . . . These past months have made me extremely aware of just how easy it is to disappear from the church. During this whole time, I have not been contacted once by any members to check in about my absences.

If a person works second shift, it is very hard to get to services and for fellowship. It has been four months for me now since I've talked to people from the church and still I wait. But I won't quit and I hope the church doesn't quit on me.

Aged or Infirm

Fourth and finally, a substantial percentage of this low or marginal group includes those who have contributed to the congregation for decades and now, because of old age and illnesses, have diminished capacities and are unable to participate. However, they often still want to be involved, and in many cases express a longing for greater connection to their church family.

I want to be more involved, however, my age and health leaves only giving and prayer for me. . . . I would like more emphasis on seniors. I feel we watch out for children and youth and the middle aged get a bulk of the planning but us seniors feel set aside sometimes.

I have been a member of this church for 63 years. . . . A few years ago I had life threatening surgery. I was four days in the critical care unit and another nine in the hospital. Then, I had three months of nurses in my home to regain strength. Many people, members of the congregation, that is, knew what was happening. I only heard from one member. I even asked another member to place me on the prayer chain and I never heard again from the church again. Just an observation that colored my desire for future fellowship.

Those with No Involvement

There is a final category of the uninvolved, one which our own surveys did not cover. Yet to complete the picture of a church's full membership they must be accounted for. These are the members who are on the rolls but haven't been seen in years or decades. In essence they have dropped out of active church involvement. Some of this group are likely deceased, retired to Florida or Arizona, or even active elsewhere.

Yet we need to consider those local people who are "mental members," a term Kirk Hadaway popularized. These persons haven't explicitly dropped their identification with their church, or their denomination, or Christianity, much less a "Christian worldview." If asked on a survey, they would identify with "Christian," and if probed would then answer "Baptist" or "Methodist," although they might have a hard time remembering the correct name of the church. They haven't kept up with the last three pastoral changes. They still "belong"—mentally in spirit but not in physical presence—and may eventually call on the church to marry their daughter or bury their loved one. They get something out of being affiliated, however loosely, with a religious community. It may be a community of memories for them, or the church is indelibly embedded in their family's heritage and story, or they could be "legacy" members—connected because of a long line of forefathers and mothers who were members.

Kirk Hadaway is one of the few persons who has engaged in research on these dropouts. He has identified three types of such "marginal members," which he calls the estranged, the indifferent, and the nominals.* The indifferent and nominal have lost all passion for and interest in organized religion. They are likely to have no church connection or membership, only a vague sense of religiosity detached from an actual congregation.

---

*Hadaway, C. K. *What Can We Do About Church Dropouts?* Nashville, TN: Abingdon Press, 1990.

As Hadaway explains the distinctions in these types, his assessment is that the estranged are the most likely to be wooed back into involvement. The estranged do not require a radical, life-changing conversion that would be necessary in order to bring the indifferent and the nominal back to church. The estranged may well be those declining participation members who were allowed to slide unheeded out the back door. Estranged members may be primarily of two types: those connected through family heritage or those with personal issues that never get addressed. For this first type, family ties keep them bound ever so tenuously to the church. For the latter type, their hurt feelings keep them tangentially connected to the congregation.

Ironically the ire of this second type of estranged members allows the door to remain open and makes them recoverable. They will seldom reengage on their own, but they are waiting for the church to act.

Still Reachable and Wanting to Be Connected

The common theme in the comments of the 80 percent of the flock who are less connected is that they express a desire to *be connected*. Even when they drag their feet, many of these people who are drifting away or are actively leaving are still doing so with ties to the church and with longings to being involved. They want to be trained and given responsibility. They want the dynamics at the church to be different, to inspire them to live out a Christian life in service. And most important they want to be spiritually fulfilled. For some, fulfillment might well be an individualistic venture, but occasionally others explicitly express a longing for the church's and the pastor's help with that quest.

> The common theme . . . of the 80 percent of the flock who are less connected is that they express a desire to *be connected.*

I'm looking for how God can use me for God's purpose here and now.

My desire is that I become more involved in the church. . . . I would like to see church officials do more to encourage us to join and be involved.

When the least involved were asked what would increase their involvement, their responses suggested that they could be reengaged if the church strengthened three things: meaningful worship, pastoral care, and ministry to the sick, shut in, and bereaved.

Such answers suggest that many needs are not being met in this group of members who are decreasing or have already diminished their involvement. Many of these needs are physical or social, but often they are intimately tied to a lack of development of members' gifts and passions or a lack of education and nurturance in a spiritually fulfilling community.

All it takes to identify these needs and yearnings is to listen, which is the focus of the following chapter.

3

HOW TO CREATE
A LISTENING TEAM

We know of a church whose district superintendent urged its leaders to undertake a serious listening exercise. The church had experienced many years of declining attendance through several different pastors.

With guidance from the district superintendent, the church board designated several members to become a listening team. After receiving training, they developed a set of about six questions. Then they spent a month publicizing the idea in the pulpit, bulletins, and mailed letters. They set up a schedule where people could sign up for forty-five-minute individual interviews during various evening, daytime, and weekend hours. The approach was for people to write their answers to the questions, and then to meet with someone from the listening team to read and explain their comments.

The questions asked people about their history with the church and their dreams for its future. They asked what problems people saw with the church and what role they could play in solving those problems. They asked how people understood the vision of the church, and how they wanted to contribute to their church's future health and growth.

Most active members took part in the process, as did a number of inactive members. Everyone seemed to appreciate the genuine efforts to listen to them.

The church board, which included many of the church's elders, spent several meetings discussing what they had heard. The pastor spent the next year working through the issues raised. The process affected the topics he preached on and led to a special prayer emphasis, a lengthy process of clarifying the church's vision and gaining wider ownership of it, and improved communication with everyone associated with the church, both active members and those more on the fringe.

Most people felt that the year-plus process was helpful and worthwhile, and in the months to follow a healthier spirit was clearly evident in the church. The church still needed to deal with its decline in attendance and finances, but now it was more ready to do so. The season of listening had made it more unified, more hopeful, more aware of its many assets, and more able to move forward to deal with these deeper issues.

Five Categories to Use

The surveys we used attempted to do roughly the same thing this church's leaders did. The surveys enabled us to listen to thousands of congregations across the United States. Before we drill down to your congregation to help you listen to it, let's review the insights we gained from listening to the full range of survey respondents.

One lesson that was loud and clear is that participation is not an either/or matter where people leap the gap from no involvement into a preestablished "ideal attender" profile. Participants cannot be divided into sheep that do everything they should or goats who don't do any of it, as Table 3.1 illustrates, perhaps comically. The pattern is more like a movement across a spectrum, from less to more involvement. In most churches every member is at a different point in that spectrum, both in where they start and in where they hope to land. The variations are affected by people's interests, time constraints, and needs. Some do "everything they should" while others might be robust attenders who don't serve or participate in small groups. Other folks may seldom show up for worship services yet give significantly, have friends in the church, and may even volunteer in

Table 3.1 Unfortunately distinguishing sheep and goats is never this easy!

Activities	Sheep	Goats
Put God first in everything	Yes	No
Heartfelt involvement at church	Yes	No
Truly live their faith	Yes	No
Hypocritical, not walking their talk	No	Yes
Fail to exercise faith	No	Yes
Choose not to contribute in any way	No	Yes

unexpected ways. The only way to know is to ask them and listen to their distinctive answers.

In Chapters One and Two we profiled five different levels of involvement. We will now review what groupings you might use before we suggest how you might identify these same categories in your own church.

The Highly Committed

These members are your ideal in terms of involvement. Interestingly this group more than others also describes itself as the most spiritually fulfilled. Not only are the highly committed most likely to respond to questionnaires, but they also volunteer to do most of the activities in the church.

This group participates for diverse reasons, and not always for the reasons that leaders assume. Therefore it is critical for a church's leadership to understand what it is that makes the highly committed different from the rest of the congregation. What is it that inspired these folks to be so highly involved? If they are cruising in high gear with all cylinders firing—to use an automotive metaphor—how did this happen? At what point in the history of the church did they connect with the church? What keeps them connected over time and through the natural changes that take place in church programs and leadership?

They are your finest calipers, measuring what is working and what is not. They are also the church's best, and worst, critics. They care. This group has the most vested interest in the health of the congregation. They may be opinionated, but it is out of an intense commitment to the vitality of the church.

> It is critical for a church's leadership to understand what it is that makes the highly committed different from the rest of the congregation.

Learn about their reasons for involvement. What rewards do they get out of their participation, and more importantly, are they completely happy doing what they do? If they feel compelled to be involved out of obligation, duty, or a suffering servant mentality, perhaps they are somewhat unhappy and really want to be doing different things. If they are serving to control church dynamics, or to maintain a family's sense of power in the community, maybe they are best retired or at least cycled off leadership for a while. If they are actively engaged because it is their only community outlet or social connection, or as a result of a psychological desire to be needed, perhaps taking them off service committees would be devastating and lead them to disconnect from the church. Regardless of their motivation, congregational leadership will not fully comprehend the dynamics of their involvement without intentionally asking and listening to them.

Those Increasing Their Participation

For the most part this group is composed of those who have made a discovery, whether it is the joy of being a new Christian, a sense of meaning and purpose, or a place to serve and use their gifts and talents. These persons are excited about their sense of fulfillment, their new levels of service or ministry. This excitement has created optimism and a spiritual energy that is felt throughout their lives and spirit and is translated into greater participation within the church.

Many of these folks come to their increased involvement through paths not always obvious to church leadership. Some develop greater connections through the encouragement of friends or trusted leaders, while others blindly respond to a general announcement. However, many of this group make the decision to be involved either out of their own desire to engage or through an inward spiritual prompting without an overt external intervention.

No matter the precipitating factor, in all cases these folks are offered the opportunity to serve and be involved; they receive encouragement and have the time, will, and energy plus the spiritual motivation. They are rewarded, even indirectly, with deeper spiritual growth through their involvement and service, which also translates into increased giving, more relationships, and inviting others.

This is one of the key groups for leaders to listen to and learn from. These people tell the current story of "what is working" in how they describe their involvement and their paths to greater participation. Theirs is a snapshot of what's working well in the church. They are—to use the car image again—accelerating and up-shifting.

How did this come about? The church leadership needs to hear why. It needs to know what is resonating with these folks organizationally and programmatically. More than any other group, those who are currently increasing their participation can teach you what your church is currently doing right.

Those Decreasing Their Participation

Those who are decreasing their participation are a congregation's warning flag. For one reason or another members of this group are distancing themselves or being disconnected from active involvement. They are more likely to express disappointment, a sense of being slighted, unhappiness with present situations, and most importantly a lack of fulfillment in their spiritual lives.

These folks have often been at the church for a long time. Some of this group are now leaving their prescribed "time of committee service," while others have needs—whether emotional or physical—that are not being met. A quarter are upset at congregational dynamics or unhappy with the pastor. They want more meaningful worship and pastoral counseling and a more caring ministry for their needs. In short they want to be heard, reached out to, and addressed on an individual basis. They are no longer the new people at church, and they now feel overlooked, uncared for, and by extension unneeded. If this dynamic continues unchecked, their one foot out the back door will soon become their entire body.

If the highly and increasingly involved groups tell the leadership what it is doing right, this group with decreasing engagement shows what the congregation is lacking, and to what degree. Not only are these people the canaries in the mine, the first to fall when the oxygen becomes weak, but they also represent the greatest potential for increasing participation within the church. This is the most important group to motivate toward participation and to keep from exiting.

The Marginally Involved

The dynamics of this group on the margins are embodied in the common saying that the opposite of love is apathy. Those members with very low involvement show few signs of being antichurch or of actively disliking congregational dynamics. However, most are not unhappy, nor are they dissatisfied. Rather, they are disconnected and neutral toward church activities and spiritual investment.

This disconnection seems to be the result of two primary conditions. One group of marginal people is relatively new to the church. They don't know what they should be doing; they don't know the church's vision or identity, and thus they have little investment or sense of belonging. In a sense they are still on the outside looking in. For some reason, they have yet to be connected, organizationally or spiritually. The other group of marginals is composed of older, longtime, and formerly involved persons. These folks have drifted into church retirement, perhaps because of illness, lack of transportation, or just a wish for bygone days when their favorite pastor was there, their pet ministry was ascendant, or their friends were alive and controlling the church. They still want to be members but have little motivation to be connected. For church leadership this group of marginal members is full of potential. What they are saying, ever so quietly on the fringe, is this: "If the church makes the effort—through communication, information, outreach, or people development—we might respond."

> What they are saying is this: "If the church makes the effort—through communication, information, outreach, or people development—we might respond."

The Uninvolved and the Missing

We heard from this group only indirectly, and thus its voices are the softest. Yet often churches strain to hear them over the louder voices within the congregation. This uninvolved group, which often masquerades among the "unchurched," is really made up of various streams of people—some of whom might even want what the church has to offer.

A few of the nominals, independents, or critics can be reached with effort, by "doing church" differently, or with sincere outreach. It is our contention that congregation leadership should save its efforts to reach these long-gone sheep until after attempting to bring a church's existing flock back into the fold. Making the effort to reach your own congregation and reinvigorate its spiritual connections may well create an excitement that becomes a natural attraction for some of the harder-to-reach, uninvolved bystanders.

In order to know the sheep on these various paths within your church you have to listen to what your members say about their involvement. A leadership team must learn the well-trod trails and also recognize the blocks that lead to members' stagnation and disengagement. A team can know this only by making an effort to hear from the full spectrum of members in the church, from the regular and active participants to the members who show up only at "high holy holiday" and "hatch and dispatch" events. If you strategize after hearing from only the most active 20 percent or so, that will be the scope of your ministry. What would your ministry be like if you listened to 100 percent of your membership? We now turn to how you might go about listening to your congregation.

Discover Your Church's Participation Quotient

As you think about your church's approach to listening, we will use the generic name "Listening Team" for the group we encourage you to form at your church. Certainly feel free to come up with your own term.

Your Listening Team's task is twofold: (1) to gain an accurate picture of your membership's (or attendance's) involvement in the congregation, and (2) to uncover the church leadership's often hidden assumptions about involvement at the church. This will require leaders to develop numerical tallies, an assessment, and potentially a recommended strategy. The Listening Team will do much of what we have modeled through our church surveys and visits, as described in the preceding chapters, but scaled in a way that is appropriate to your church.

The Listening Team

Who should be on the Listening Team that is committing to this churchwide engagement process? The number of people on this team depends on the size of the church and the participants' available time. While the pastor could be part of the team, we encourage as much qualified lay involvement as possible. Whether or not the church's pastor(s) are involved, they must be fully committed to what the team is seeking to accomplish and to any needed changes that are identified as feedback is accumulated from various people associated with the church.

Smaller Churches. Persons asked to join this team should be genuine, sincere, caring, and people-oriented. They may be deacons, pastoral counselors, Stephen Ministry caregivers (www .stephenministries.org), or members of hospitality or greeting teams. They should love their church and care deeply about congregational members.

Once composed, this group should be trained on the purpose of their task. They are to reach out to members and listen to how they are doing. They are acting as ambassadors for the church in a process of checking in with *all* members, if possible, or with *anyone* locally associated with the church. In their visits they may need to acknowledge a lack of personal contact by church leadership, lament this shortcoming, and stress an interest in all members, which the church leadership has resolved to renew.

The goal of these visits is to reestablish a connection and listen to members as they describe their family life, involvement expectations, and any needs or desires they have regarding the church. Team members are to generally assess respondents' interest in deepening their connections with the church. The essence of these conversations as well as facts about life changes, health, church friendships, observed needs, and so on should remain confidential. Any corrections in family information (deaths, divorces, children at college, address updates, and so forth) should be clearly recorded. It should be clear at all times that these efforts are to reach out to members and attenders, to whom the church has a spiritual responsibility, rather than spy on persons to collect fodder for marketing or gossip.

Larger Churches. The ideal with larger churches is to do what smaller churches do: connect personally and individually with everyone associated with the church. However, in larger congregations (or even smaller ones with a high percentage of nonattending members) this ideal might be unrealistic to consider. Instead the team might determine to visit only a sampling of members to uncover patterns rather than attempt to reestablish ties. Or a church may opt for a congregational survey and a gifts/skills assessment, and then pour its energy into ensuring as close to a 100-percent response as possible.

Members who are engaged in the church are easier to connect with. If half of a church's members are already engaged participants, it is relatively straightforward to assess satisfaction with involvement, judge the level of burnout or enthusiasm for volunteering, and determine needs for additional leadership training among the congregation. However, if for example 70 percent of the membership is disengaged, the same tasks may be quite daunting.

Other strategies for listening to the needs of members might include small-group meetings, cottage groups, focus groups, or visits to naturally occurring groups and committees in the church. Keep in mind that any effort to uncover involvement dynamics that entails an individual's voluntary participation will miss many persons who are less engaged. In this listening process it is the least committed and those currently diminishing their participation that you especially need to hear from.

If the church is quite large, a questionnaire sent to all names associated with the congregation may be necessary. Appendix C contains questions that could be used for such a survey.

However you conduct this congregational listening effort, the outcome should primarily attempt to uncover the patterns of involvement within the membership and identify the hindrances to participation. The effort should also strive to correct the membership listing and ideally enhance it with notations about the interests of members, their needs, their gifts and skills, pastoral care actions needed, and so on.

Tools You Will Need

Early on in the Listening Team's process you will need to develop a list of people to contact, whether for visits, phone calls, or surveys. Perhaps start with existing data that the church currently collects. Is there a membership list? If so, how accurate is it? Is there a database of people who live locally and who have been associated with the church in some way? Some churches have separate membership listings for those who give financially, for volunteer involvement, or for worship service attendance. Try to combine those lists to generate an initial profile of member participation.

It might also be helpful to produce a map of the home location of members during this initial data-gathering phase. There are several computer programs, some free, that will help you create a map of where various people in your congregation live. Appendix A lists a few such resources.

Confidentiality Is Critical

Before it gets too far, your Listening Team will need to talk about what to keep confidential and how to do this. This process involves your team's conversations as well as your records, since you will be dealing with sensitive personal information. Any material produced or collected should be locked away from accidental observation by those not engaged in this sensitive task. If possible, perhaps all records on individuals might use identifying numbers from a secure database rather than actual names.

Think too about how your team will be regarded as others imagine what you are doing. A slip of the tongue or careless comment could turn a worthy venture into gossipmongering, or worse. The damage might create a breech of trust, conflict, or the departure of members.

Agree on an "elevator speech"—a credible and helpful description of what you are doing, short enough that you could voice it on an elevator ride. A truthful public statement could be, "We are reaching out and listening to everyone in the church, from the most active to the least active." Or, "The church board created a short-term Listening Team who will try to help the church's leadership improve its understanding of the congregation's needs." A recipe for failure is any buzz that distorts what you are doing: "Pastor has some buddies grading the church based on how much people give or how much they support his programs." Even worse would be, "A secret group is classifying everyone in the church as a sheep or a goat."

As you create written documents, try to anticipate how they will be used, and design them accordingly. Will any of your data, such as corrected phone numbers or e-mail addresses, go into the church database or software? Is it possible that some of your findings will need to be shared with pastoral care visitation teams for further visits, and if so, could you use a format that will be helpful for that group?

In everything you do, keep in mind that the ultimate goal of this process is increased participation and enhanced spiritual development.

Publicizing the Listening Effort

The Listening Team's existence could be publicly described as an intentional churchwide effort to reconnect with all members. This intention could also be signaled through the church's announcements, newsletter, individual letters, or e-mail distribution. Several sermons could be dedicated to the topic of caring for all the children of God, or the meaning of membership, or even the marks of a Christian life. Signal the sincere intention of the church leadership to renew, and in some cases restore, relations with all members in an effort to nurture the spiritual development of the flock.

The long-term success of the overall process rests on church leadership becoming more intentional about tracking the participation of each member. This can happen in many ways, but however the church chooses a plan, it should be put into place at the beginning of the listening process. We suggest using a simple database or spread-sheet. Table 3.2 offers one model, but do tailor it to match your situation. Use it to track family characteristics, personal interests and skills, attendance, involvement in committees, ministry efforts, and participation in educational and training events. Some may balk at the detail we are suggesting. Indeed we are encouraging an ideal, but it is also important to remember that if spiritual leaders are charged with the care of their members' souls, then they must be well informed to do this with accuracy. Establishing some method of record-keeping is critical at the outset of this listening effort.

> The Listening Team's existence could be publicly described as an intentional churchwide effort to reconnect with all members.

Part of the Listening Team's confidential role is to reflect on the underlying assumptions that the church's leadership—key influencers from pastor(s) to board(s)—has about participation. These assumptions include the expectations they think they're conveying, and the assumed process for how people become involved. Our research (see Chapter Six) indicated quite disjunctive models at work when we compared staff attitudes about pathways toward involvement against what members actually said and did. In other words the various ways members became involved and their patterns of participation in the church were completely different from staff expectations and assumptions. Members used many paths to church participation, whereas staff mostly assumed one set route.

Table 3.2 Your listening team will need a confidential format to record its notes

Confidential Notes from Listening Team Visits/Interviews
(Before meeting, try to obtain as much information as possible from church records)

Contact Information and Demographics
Last name
First name
Street address
City, state, zip
Home phone
Cell phone
E-mail
Age
Marital status
Children or other family issues

Roles in Church
Year came

What they initially liked about the church

What they like most about church today

Closest friends in the church

Initial involvement, if any

Recent involvement, if any

Financial donor to church

Helpful Background
Personal interests

Skills

Professional background

Spiritual gifts

Other relevant education and training

Confidential Assessment of Involvement Level (check one)
☐ Highly committed
☐ Increasing participation
☐ Decreasing participation
☐ Marginally involved
☐ Uninvolved or missing

Other Comments

Also church leaders' assumptions about what constituted "good" participation differed widely from what members perceived as good church citizenship. In other words staff saw participation in an idealistic, cumulative model, whereas participants had many starting points and selectively picked and chose their type and level of participation on the basis of their needs rather than on a model of involvement.

Getting leadership and staff's implicit assumptions out in the open will facilitate hearing clearly how members talk about their involvement. Listeners need to hear what members actually say rather than framing what they hear into their own predetermined categories. It is important to realize that such categories, assumptions, and "ideal" models are operative within the leadership. They may represent cherished and theologically sound paths, but they can also be barriers to members' increased involvement. One group's preferred path can be a hindrance to others' efforts to reach their goal. Recognizing these assumptions doesn't mean that they should be discarded; rather these expectations should be "put on the shelf" in order to objectively and compassionately hear the stories of members as you begin to listen to them talk about their level of involvement in the church.

Putting Everything Together

Once the many notes and lists have been collected, the core leadership team should collectively and honestly evaluate the participation level of each church member. This could well be a difficult and anxiety-producing task. Since elementary school, few of us have been fond of receiving grades or having our performance judged. Nevertheless an accurate assessment of current involvement levels is critical. This evaluation does not need to be detailed at first. But you will find it helpful to have an overall numerical assessment of the core participants, those recently increasing or decreasing their involvement, those marginally connected to the life of the church, and those long gone or dearly departed (and perhaps remove these from the list). Table 3.3 shows a very simple example of the confidential summary that the Listening Team might create.

In smaller churches this might be a relatively easy task; however, larger churches may have to tolerate some gaps or unknowns at this point. Either way, these numbers will be helpful in determining follow-on steps for the Listening Team as well as for the church's senior leadership.

What does the spectrum of participation look like in your church? Are truly 20 percent of the members doing most of the work? Perhaps you have 40 or 50 percent involved at some level and a core of 5 or 10 percent offering leadership?

This profile of participation becomes a guide for how to proceed. If participation is relatively high, then the task will be primarily to reassess current volunteering and then target the marginal and uninvolved members. The basic structures of groups and congregational life might be quite healthy. However, if the church's involvement percentage is low, a more intensive effort may be necessary. Not only would there be more need for individualized outreach, but serious consideration might have to be given to the church's efforts at promoting participation. Perhaps the entire church will need teaching on the characteristics of a committed Christian life or efforts at raising the bar on

Table 3.3 Your listening team should create a confidential overall tally

Groups in the Church	Estimated Percentage	Comments
Highly committed		
Those increasing their participation		
Moderately involved		
Those decreasing their participation		
Marginally involved		
Uninvolved or missing		
	TOTAL: 100%	

involvement. A reconsideration of the volunteer culture at the church, and perhaps a radical reconfiguration of the leadership and committee and group memberships may need to take place before growth in participation will increase.

Learning Beyond the Membership

This book is based on the ideas of listening to those who made the shift from spectator to disciple and of exploring the ways others might make a similar shift, especially those we are calling the other 80 percent. As the Listening Team reaches out to woo and engage missing sheep, they should report back to the senior leadership of the church so that they can understand the dynamics of those who have departed. That task will be helped by realizing that there are other factors at work in our modern world which diminish commitment and hinder involvement. For that we must not only listen to our membership but also learn about the world they live in. This is explored in the next part of the book.

Part Two

LEARNING

Listening to the people of your church (Part One) helps you understand the reasons why some folks are already very committed and involved in community, why some are moving in that direction, why some are traveling the opposite way, and why some behave as spectators only and haven't moved at all.

Listening helps, but it won't give you all the answers you need to address the dynamic of marginal commitment and involvement in the group we're calling the other 80 percent. The fact is that the problem doesn't rest solely in unwilling or dissatisfied people. Some issues require you to look beyond your people. Part Two, on *learning*, seeks to gain an even bigger picture on other dynamics at work that prevent "the other 80 percent" from being involved. These insights provide additional perspective and tools needed to turn your church's spectators into active disciples.

Chapter Four explores how changes in society compound the problem. It covers issues like the changing meanings of words and the general decline in commitment to organizations. Chapter Five investigates how church structures and programs either hinder or promote involvement. Chapter Six looks at how staff expectations and their "planned" paths into the life of the church can actually hinder a large percentage of members from connecting at a deep level. It's like having one or two doors open but folks are lining up at the locked doors they would prefer to come in through.

Chapter Seven then invites you to create a "learning team" for your own church. In doing so, you identify the various larger cultural, societal, and sociological issues that play into the 80/20 problem.

The book's final chapters (Part Three) will suggest specific ways to *lead* your people into greater involvement based on what you have gained from listening to your congregation and learning from the influences outside of the congregation.

4

CULTURAL CAUSES OF
THE 80/20 PROBLEM

Changes in society and culture have significantly complicated the challenge of involvement levels at church. We saw this vividly when we went to Austin, Texas, to study a church there. We arrived very early Sunday morning to watch the set-up team transform the local high school in which the church was to assemble. We stayed until early evening, meeting with different church people and observing various ministries. Each of us spent more hours that day "at church" than on any previous day in our lives!

Our day included a few stretch breaks outdoors and two short drives to nearby restaurants for meals. As we viewed the landscape around the site where the church was meeting, we were amazed at the competition the church faced on Sunday mornings—as probably most churches do.

First, even getting to the high school was a bit challenging since there was a 10K run that morning to raise money and awareness for a charity. The route for the run was cordoned off in front of the school, giving worshipers quite a challenge to reach their intended destination.

The high school also bordered a public park along a river. In the morning we watched easily a hundred people unload their boats, fishing rods, picnic blankets, kites, Frisbees, bicycles, and other gear for a happy day at the park. Many seemed to come as families.

The school also had two athletic fields. All day long we saw people of all ages come and go to soccer games.

Our lunch spot was at a restaurant across the street from the entrance to the high school property. As we stood in line outside the restaurant waiting for a seat, we could see signs across the street welcoming people to the church services. We wanted to tell diners that the church didn't have a waiting line, and that the music was far better than what the restaurant was playing.

As we drove back to the high school, we saw a couple of yard sales in front of various homes. Truly this town, as most, offered many appealing alternatives to church.

In yesteryear, community life paused during church hours and even protected them. Not today! If Sunday morning in our culture is no longer sacred time set aside for going to church, it's not for sleeping either.

Some Changes Are Obvious, but More Are Subtle

The big issue of this chapter is that changes are taking place in society and culture that hinder commitment and participation in a church. The subtle changes are the hardest to spot. Church leaders need to be aware of these changes as they try to lead churchgoers to become more involved. This is not to blame, excuse, or propose a compromise. Rather it is the social reality churches must deal with.

As the world changes, which it certainly has been doing throughout Christian history, church leaders must continually assess culture's effect on how they present the unchanging Gospel message. Shifts have taken place in the role "church" plays in our society, including the reasons we would want to become members and what we hope and expect to get out of our involvement. Each of these societal trends affects how people approach their commitment to church. For example, in an era of consumer-driven culture, a church's worship style is beginning to take precedent over its denominational ties. Commitment to something that fulfills "my" spiritual needs now trumps membership simply because of a long-established family heritage.

Likewise in an era that highly prizes choice, fulfillment of "my" spiritual needs trumps the idea of fulfilling the obligations of my church's committee structure. I may be just what the XYZ Committee needs, but if it doesn't fulfill me personally, I'm likely to say no, even if someone in church authority specifically asks me to be part of it.

Many churches have not responded adequately to this changing context. In part it is due to a desire to hold on to the past, to conserve the old-time religion that was good enough for one's grandparents. But in part it is also due to our commitment to deeper issues; often we conceive church and Christianity one way while society has moved past our constructs of social reality.

One regrettable outcome of these societal changes is that faith in Christ is not widely perceived as an active lifestyle that one attempts to live out every day in all one's actions. Rather faith has become something that one can assent to but does not live, believe but does not follow, and belong to but does not support or participate in. Too many people willingly go to church on Sunday, but during the week they are involved in sex outside of marriage, are dishonest at work, or are unforgiving toward a sibling.

> Faith has become something that one can assent to but does not live, believe but does not follow, and belong to but does not support or participate in.

It would be wrong to say that this problem comes only with wayward sheep or even from poor shepherding. Here are several cultural shifts and their implications for church involvement.

Eroding Traditional Connections

In yesteryear the world was more local, and church life was close to the center. Family ties and community solidarity often reinforced church attendance and participation. In many people's

worldview church attendance was certainly a religious matter, but it was also a civic and family-related reality as well.
In many American towns, churches were built at the central
crossroads, symbolizing their important place in the community. They often served as gathering points for civic meetings
as well.

Today's towns and cities rarely promote that level of connection. Instead they are more diverse—religiously, ethnically,
and culturally. People are also more mobile. Fewer live near
extended family. You might see your sister or cousin at church
but certainly not the entire clan. Now when the clan does
gather for holidays or summer get-togethers, people must travel
to do so, creating yet another situation where regular attenders
miss church.

Further today's multiple family configurations of step-families
add another pull away from church. If a parent is driving an hour
to pick up the kids on an every-other-weekend basis, church attendance and involvement often suffer.

It is no secret that an increasing number of households
now have two wage earners. Or perhaps one person has taken
an additional part-time job to make ends meet. This too pulls
against church involvement as people do activities on weekends
that they used to do on weekdays. They may also have jobs that
require them to work during church hours.

Married couples today are also waiting longer to have children and working longer before retirement. Both circumstances
reduce potential volunteer time. Almost thirty years ago, for a
church interview Warren did during college, he traveled to
a small Pennsylvania town to report on a church that was
bursting at the seams. "I can't wait to retire so I'll have more
time for my church," Warren remembers one man telling him,
indicating that church was his primary social outlet. "There are
so many more ways I want to volunteer at here." In the decades
since, as society has changed, Warren has not heard a comment
like that again.

Likewise as cities enlarge, sprawling into extensive suburbs, commutes to work become longer. We both know people who travel two hours each way into work, every day! These ever-lengthening commutes, often motivated by a desire to give their families a better life, come with the trade-off of having less time for religion.

All of these societal changes are slowly eroding traditional connections that used to reinforce the church as central to family life. Less and less do you see church as the center of extended family involvement.

Blurring of Religious Distinctiveness

A hundred years ago, if a Lutheran immigrant from Sweden married a Lutheran immigrant from Germany, it raised eyebrows and was called a mixed marriage (same if an Italian Catholic married an Irish Catholic). "What will they eat?" observing family members would say, commenting on the difference in foods the groups typically ate. "And how will they celebrate the Christmas?" another frowning family observer might ask, as customs differed considerably across ethnic lines, even among European Lutherans.

In recent years many surveys have tracked the rise in switching denominations, such as from Methodist to Assemblies of God, or from Episcopal to nondenominational. This happens in marriages as when a Baptist marries a Presbyterian and one of them changes. Or they go "church shopping" and decide they both like the fast-growing church in town, so they together become whatever it is. Likewise interfaith marriages are on the rise, as when a Protestant marries a Catholic, a Jew, a Mormon, or someone who has no religion and wants to keep it that way.

Robert Putnam and David Campbell's book *American Grace* (see Bibliography) documents this trend but also points out the "Aunt Susan" effect. Increasingly, Putnam says, we all have a relative who we like and respect but is of a different faith.

The net result of these changes around us is a growing willingness to cross denominational boundaries, and a weakening of denominational identity and loyalty. Religious brands lose their distinctiveness.

The implications for church participation and involvement are major. People are increasingly willing to move to another church (or faith) rather than remain loyal and invest deeply in one. If one church isn't immediately convenient or does something irksome, then moving on is rather easy if you view other traditions as equally acceptable. As a result fewer people today become woven into the fabric of their congregation.

> Fewer people today become woven into the fabric of their congregation.

Increasing Individualism

Almost any purchase today can be customized to fit an individual's needs. Scott's Lawn Service can e-mail you every two weeks to advise on what you should be doing (and buying) for your yard, on the basis of your climate and recent temperatures. Amazon.com tailors book recommendations for each individual. Blue jeans can be special-ordered to fit your body perfectly. A machine at the shoe store analyzes your foot issues exactly and selects the correct orthotics and pair of shoes. Beds can be ordered with two different custom settings, one for each spouse.

Is it any surprise that this consumer-driven focus on how to create self-fulfillment for "my needs" has come to church? Commitment has always been a reciprocal exchange idea that we commit to and participate in because we receive rewards that roughly parallel what we contribute. But now the exchange is becoming more an obvious and conscious investment. Previously church involvement was tempered with family, social obligations, and subtle investments in creating social capital, bonding with neighbors, or solidifying business contacts. Increasingly these motivations have eroded to a purer exchange that must benefit me—the individual—and lead to the critical exchange question, "How does this church meet my spiritual needs?"

Desacralizing Sacred Time

In this chapter's opening illustration of the church in Austin, we affirmed that Sunday is no longer set apart as sacred. One factor that encroaches on Sunday's special place is the economy. With the demise of many blue laws, shops and malls are open all weekend, as are online consumer activities.

Financial issues are not the only factor tugging away at Sunday's sacredness. Today worship services also face stiff competition from sports events, sports leagues for adults and children, adult leisure groups, television, movies, and extended family get-togethers. The U.S. Postal Service may not deliver mail on Sundays, but smart phones, texting, and e-mail take its place, competing for any quiet time remaining on Sundays.

Today church seems somehow to be in direct competition with the time spent with family. When the issue is framed that way, sports and academic achievement for your children and other family needs nearly always win out.

Declining Civic Engagement

Robert Putnam's *Bowling Alone: The Collapse and Revival of American Community* (see Bibliography) chronicles declining civic engagement and social connectedness over three decades. He presents evidence of how membership in hundreds of social organizations like bowling leagues has diminished dramatically during this time. One outcome is the fraying of our informal ties with friends, neighbors, and relatives. In 1975 the average American entertained friends at home fifteen times per year; the equivalent figure in recent years is barely half that, according to Putnam. Virtually all leisure activities that involve doing something with someone else, from playing volleyball to playing chamber music, are declining, he says.

Putnam notes that the loss of organizational membership, such as in a bowling league, doesn't do away with the necessity of social togetherness, what he calls bridging and bonding capital. Now more than ever, he says, human beings need to make commitments that bring them into physical contact with other persons. Perhaps as never before, physical, tangible, and meaningful commitments must be called for and nurtured—including at church.

Church Contributions to the Problem

Changes in society and cultural norms may hinder commitment and participation, creating pressures that make people less willing to volunteer. These and other patterns in our changing world require the church to reconfigure how it talks about involvement. This need is clearly seen in the way congregations conceptualize membership. Additionally, the idea that attendance is a primary goal must also be reconsidered.

Emphasis on Membership

A good first step is to start with the word *membership*, since it is by far the most widely used category for those who have made a commitment to the church.

How can the idea of "membership" itself be part of the problem? We probably all agree that Jesus didn't recruit volunteers or members in the sense many people today use those words; he called people to be his disciples. Yet most people in our churches are drawn to terms like *member* and *volunteer*. Many understand these terms in ways that are far below biblical standards.

In part it's because of what our surrounding culture is teaching us. It sends messages that affect how people think—church leaders included. Thus it is very important to gauge what your congregation means when its individuals hear and use certain words like *membership* and *volunteer*. If they have heard "membership has its privileges" all week from American Express ads, won't that influence how they feel about church "membership"? If they were just recruited for a neighborhood service project by hearing the oft-used pitch that "in volunteer work the dividends are always greater than the investment," won't that color the expectations they bring to volunteering at church?

This issue of language matters because people measure themselves against whatever ideal or standard they (or you) have emphasized most. Sometimes they're not even aware of these often unwritten ideals or standards, but they register all the same. It's like those television ads that we think we are ignoring, until later, when we're hungry, we find ourselves heading over to the food chain whose advertisement we thought we had tuned out.

Membership in an organization is an idea from an earlier generation when, like social class, it was accompanied by a certain lifestyle and associated with strong societal expectations. Today church membership is more of a status marker but frequently without much measurable substance beyond perhaps the initial "I do" of joining. It's often a badge we wear to label our tradition ("I'm Presbyterian") rather than a spiritual commitment and covenant that we live out. It is an "ascribed identity" based on our birth, family heritage, or traditional norms rather than an "achieved identity" we've intentionally chosen, striven to acquire, and in part even actively helped create. At best, membership is an anchor that keeps us from drifting too far from a past commitment rather than being a vital personal identity that bestows a vision and sense of purpose that directs our ongoing daily path and actions.

Warren belonged to a church that was sued on trumped-up charges by one of its members. The member had been arrested that year for beating his wife. He hadn't attended services for over a year. He didn't give any money to the church. He had refused to meet with the elders. Yet his lawsuit claimed that he was a "member in good standing." A judge would agree because many years previous the man did go through a membership class and had said "I do" to certain values and beliefs. Legally he was presumed to be a member in good standing unless the church could prove otherwise.

Maybe that's an extreme example, but could it be that many others in that church feel likewise? Too many people feel they're members in good standing, even if they have no current relationship with the church and show no progress in their spiritual lives. That should not happen.

> Too many people feel they're members in good standing, even if they have no current relationship with the church and show no progress in their spiritual lives.

By contrast Scott recently had a conversation with the pastor of a rapidly growing multiracial, charismatic congregation in New England who conveyed a very different conception of membership. Almost half of the attenders have become members after a very demanding initiation: each committed to sacrificial financial giving, attended extensive new-member classes, agreed to serve in the church's ministries, was screened extensively by church leadership, and accepted a detailed theological statement after proving that he or she knew what it meant. Even under such rigorous criteria the pastor commented that the more stringent the leadership makes the membership requirements, the more those who attend want to make the effort to reach that goal. In other words the higher this church sets the member criteria bar, the more people strive to reach it.

A recent news article looked at what might be labeled as the radical membership sermons of Rick Warren at Saddleback Church and Craig Groschel at LifeChurch, two of today's most visible pastors and churches. Both messages call for increasing levels of commitment, even to the point of telling people to find another church if they don't want to rise to the challenge. As Rick Warren said in his sermon, "If you're in this church, I'm coming after you to be mobilized."*

Both preachers affirmed that everyone is a minister and is expected to be actively involved in discipleship. These high-profile sermons make the point that "being a Christian" matters in daily activities, and it costs. Certainly this is not a new concept, as the New Testament is full of references to the cost of discipleship, not to mention the entire history of the Christian church and the martyrdom of saintly people throughout the centuries. In contrast to most kinds of membership today, Scripture identifies a person as a "member of the body of Christ" by the ongoing work of the Holy Spirit, not by a decision on the part of the individual or the church. The Bible, such as Romans 12:5 and 1 Corinthians 12:27, repeatedly teaches membership in the sense that we are members in Christ's family to one another.

Just how far are some people's ideas of membership from the original meaning of biblical phrases like, "we are members of Christ's body" and "we are members of God's household"? In a society dominated by technology, be it the internet, video games, texting, Twitter, and online social networking arenas, our ties with each other are often virtual, impersonal, and fleeting. Each of us is able to "friend" and "follow" someone without contact, without actual engagement. Likewise if people offend us, we are able to "unfriend" them with a click and they don't even have to know that we've shunned them. For most Americans, today's world fragments our tangible social contacts and isolates our existence so that life is increasingly mediated through a screen—which makes commitment, engagement, participation, and personal sacrifice all totally optional.

---

*Ken Gurley, "Megachurch Pastor to Fake Christians: 'Get Out!'" *Houston Chronicle*, May 25, 2010 (www.chron.com/channel/houstonbelief/commons/persona.html).

Yet we suspect the spiritual parallels are very influential. Being a "fan" of an organization on Facebook no more defines our character than being an absentee member of a congregation shapes our virtues and develops our beliefs. These marginal commitments on our part may indeed provide markers for our class consciousness, traditional convictions, and musical tastes. They may even inform others of our stated and cherished ideals, but they are a world apart from getting up early to practice with the worship team, serving in a soup kitchen, volunteering in a mentoring program with disadvantaged children, or leading a support group or small-group Bible study. No amount of watching golf on television or playing Wii golf will bring us into personal relationship with Jack Nicklaus. Being a fan of rock bands won't get us into one. Nor will being a member of a church get anyone into heaven or guarantee that our relationships and character will become more Christlike. Yet it's easy to start thinking that way without even realizing it.

Our recommendation is that you come up with a new word for membership if your people see membership primarily as an organizational affiliation, or a badge of belonging to a denominational heritage, a community of memory, or the community of saints. Likewise if they understand membership in a certain local church primarily as defining certain privileges, such as being allowed to use the chapel for a relative's wedding, then indeed this concept of membership should die. And certainly if they consider membership the marker of whether or not they're a Christian, then you need to change terms. Any concept that substitutes for or lets one off the hook from the duty of being an ongoing participant in the local assembly, or an active and engaged Christian believer, should be replaced.

We honestly don't care what term you end up using in your church to represent the process of sanctification, of growing in grace, building one's faith, maturing spiritually, and becoming more like Christ. Whatever word or phrase you teach your congregation, it should convey to them a higher standard than making a one-time affirmation and then drifting away, satisfied that they now have a ticket to eternal salvation.

We urge you to reserve the category of membership (or whatever term you select) for higher criteria than the ability to sign one's name on a dotted line—figuratively or literally. If you do use the term *membership*, attach it only to those who are active, participating, and growing toward spiritual maturity of head and heart. All along remember that changes in society have trained people to have a different understanding of the word.

Finally whatever term your people know best, that's what they will consider to be the highest goal. That's where the 80/20 principle kicks in. Roughly 20 percent of the people in church engage in what following Christ means. As the book's subtitle emphasizes, the other 80 percent don't seem to. But they are worth pursuing and inviting to do so, even as Jesus affirmed that a good shepherd makes the effort to go after the wayward sheep.

Counting Attendees as a Primary Measure

Some churches go in a different direction. They eschew the category of membership altogether and focus solely on attendance. Those who show up are the ones who count; they define the congregation. From that point of view these leaders convey the idea that as long as the attendance numbers are going up, the congregation is healthy and spiritually growing.

This approach also causes difficulties. The first issue to sort out is how you count: does attendance mean coming every week? What about those who come once a month? What about those who are actively involved in the congregation's social ministries but seldom attend worship? And what about those who can't show up, such as the longtime faithful elderly person who once received a "perfect attendance" award from Sunday school but is now bedridden and contributes only a few dollars a year? Or what about the need to shepherd the students away at college, the snow birds gone to Arizona or Florida for half the year, and the traveling businesspersons who spend periods of the year away from the congregation but support it financially and are actively engaged in communication and fellowship with friends and regulars at the church?

> You cannot help people grow spiritually if you are nowhere near them, but be careful not to equate attendance with the end goal.

We wouldn't raise this point if we hadn't come across many examples of pastors who seem to equate warm bodies with spiritually growing people. Certainly you cannot help people grow spiritually if you are nowhere near them, but be careful not to equate attendance with the end goal.

Emphasizing attendance as the highest goal is thus fraught with difficulties similar to those arising when membership is emphasized as the highest goal. The latter creates a club mentality; one can join and then not feel obliged to attend. Stressing attendance can create a situation where one feels that coming is important, but it stops there. Both can create an expectation of watching a "good show"—a passive spectator mentality that trumps full involvement.

Other Contributors to the Problem

Another church-related part of this problem shows up when spiritual leadership is willing to perpetuate a conception of Christianity that is Sunday-based and minimalist rather than a seven-day-a-week lifestyle. A similar problem is the often latent assumption by church leaders that conversion to Christianity is an all-or-nothing, singular event rather than a lifetime process of sanctification.

Finally the acceptance of "church shopping" and "members as consumers," that is, people looking for church only to meet their needs, is both part of the problem but also potentially part of the solution, as will be suggested in Chapter Nine. If you set up an exchange mentality—come for our great programs to meet your needs—and then don't meet those needs, people will shop for a better deal elsewhere.

Keep Listening for the Good Shepherd

In most cases you cannot buck the tide from outside of culture. Churches will succeed in making disciples of Jesus Christ only as they proclaim Christ's teachings in words and social contexts that people can truly understand. The best communicators speak not only the language of their audience (English to English speakers) but also its cultural nuances (such as 2011 hipster English to 2011 English-speaking hipsters). By knowing about changes in society that may have an effect, whether direct or indirect, on members' involvement, you can overcome those effects.

Embrace the reality that most of your people face. Realize that time with family, baseball practices, work commutes, and the like are the challenges they have to overcome or solve in order to be more involved at church. Keep showing how God can use their involvement at church to satisfy their spiritual needs. Chapters Eight and Nine will offer more guidance on how to do this.

But don't leave them there. Christianity is also counter-cultural, and faith norms are not identical with societal norms. Meet people where they are, but don't leave them there. Move them to reconsider and reevaluate time commitments, overdone sports expectations, excess consumerism, and other destructive cultural impulses. This will help them make the space to be more involved.

Above all teach them to listen to the Good Shepherd's voice. In John 10, Jesus says he is the Good Shepherd. Five different times these verses stress the importance of listening to him. In that same passage Jesus also warns about other voices who try to entice sheep away from the Good Shepherd. The more your people know the Good Shepherd, the more they can identify the false, competing voices that come from our culture today.

5

COMPARATIVE PATTERNS IN CHURCHES

One of Scott's earliest memories of church is in vacation Bible school playing the hand game "Here is the church, here is the steeple, open the doors and see all the people." It was ingrained in his mind as far back as he could remember that the congregation, the physical gathering of the community of saints, was the "Church." As independent Baptists, this church did not subscribe to any denominational hierarchy; they proudly proclaimed a congregationalist polity in which each collection of saints had autonomy but also participated in the church universal. Years later as a member of another Baptist church, Scott remembers a sign hung on the front of the building proclaiming, "Oakhurst Baptist Church meets here." It was the coming together of the people that made the faith, not the organization or its structure.

Scott has moved beyond those congregations, but he has never left the conviction that the gathered community encompasses what it means to be a Christian. At the same time, the programs, routines, and physical reality of the organization all have a powerful formative effect on those who gather.

As sociologists of religion both authors of this book strongly affirm the importance and power of the physical organizational form that is called a church. The people constitute the congregation, the worshiping community, but the church's structural reality acts back on what takes place inside it.

In short there is more to opening the doors than just seeing all the people.

In Chapter Four we discussed the larger social context and its formative effects on participation. Here we turn to comparative patterns across churches from a national study of Protestant churches, asking how certain organizational realities—size, denomination, worship format, and so on—help or hinder church participation and volunteer recruitment.

Organizational Factors Related to Participation

We park in a distant section of the parking lot where a ministry volunteer directs us. We are part of a long line with a few dozen other cars. Soon we walk toward a large structure following countless signs reading, "This way to the worship center." Entering one of the twenty-three doors to the church, we are greeted by several smiling faces. As long as we look like we know what we are doing, they offer us a bulletin packet, and we are free to wander. We head in different directions. Our ushers point out empty seats, and we slip into large, comfy seats in the state-of-the-art sanctuary, which is darkened a bit for the projection screens running announcements as the praise band plays softly. We enjoy the service along with 3,500 other worshipers and then depart, following the masses to the exit and then to our car and the long line of other cars returning to suburbia.

In a different time, and different place, one of us (Scott) heads downtown, navigates city traffic (even on a Sunday morning), and has to circle the historic church three times before finding a parking space. Thankfully the city doesn't charge for street parking on Sundays. Walking up to the massive red front doors, I notice a sign saying welcome, but I see no one. There is noise and a few folks at a rear side door about half a block away, but I can't get there from here; so, pushing open the door, I enter. I'm a bit surprised to be joyfully greeted by a pleasant older woman, who happily notes that I am a visitor and that she is glad to see me. This is a huge building, so I wonder how she knows that I'm a visitor until I enter a second set of doors and find that the massive sanctuary, capable of seating four hundred, has about seventy-five mostly sixty-plus-year-old folks scattered throughout the auditorium. During the organ prelude I'm introduced to three persons—elders, I suspect. I get many smiles from others, and I'm asked to sign an attendance card and drop it in the offering plate. I get acknowledged as a visitor during the service, even having to stand while every eye in the place turns my way. Following the service, I'm personally asked to coffee hour, which lasts almost that long, and am engaged in several conversations, including one with the minister. When I finally make it back to my car, I feel as if I have met the entire congregation.

Size Does Make a Difference

Of course neither of these stories is fully representative of all churches their size. Scott has never been welcomed more fully by a church than when he visited the largest one in the world, Yoido Full Gospel Church in Seoul, Korea. And both of us have endured our share of, cold, inhospitable congregations that were small.

A church's size does not determine warmth and friendliness, but it does influence whether one will be noticed or not. No matter how unfriendly the congregation may be, I can't hide among forty-three attenders, while even the best welcome team in the world can easily miss someone wanting to be unnoticed among 4,300 excitedly engaged bodies streaming into a worship center that has multiple entrances.

The larger the church, the less likely one is to stand out, to be greeted, to connect, and to participate. Small churches win this competition hands down. While large churches need more volunteers to operate, in fact they need a smaller percentage of the total membership

A church's size does not determine warmth and friendliness, but it does influence whether one will be noticed or not.

Table 5.1 The smaller the church, the more of its total affiliation who actually attend

Reported Size of Congregation Based on Number of Adult Participants	Mean Percentage of All Participants Who Are Sunday Attenders
1–49	63%
50–99	59%
100–149	57%
150–349	53%
350–999	47%
1000+	45%

Source: Faith Communities Today 2000 (FACT2000), Protestants only.

to do so. Likewise as a result of greater resources, more paid staff, and the efficiency of scale, they may actually need fewer voluntary participants per member. Additionally, larger size increases the "crowd" and introduces a well-established principle of social psychology called the bystander effect, whereby the more people in a group, the less likely any one person is to act or volunteer, because the assumption is that others will act.

Thus as church size increases, so does the likelihood that persons will be spectators and free-riders in the organization. This group reluctance is also evident in attendance patterns, according to data from one study depicted in Table 5.1 (see also Table 2, in the Introduction, which shows similar data from a different study*). As the church gets larger, the leadership can expect a smaller percentage of members to show up regularly.

However, very large churches have attempted to counter this dynamic by increasing the opportunities for participation through multiple ministries, service activities, and small-group efforts. Likewise recent developments in creating multiple locations of worship for a single church also increase the demand for participation to deliver the diversified services.

*National Congregations Study.

Smaller congregations are intimate, close-knit gatherings that solidify relationships, and increase accountability and familiarity. As such they generally have a significantly greater percentage of attender-to-member involvement. Additionally the smaller the church, the less likely it is to have a full-time minister or paid staff to do the necessary work. While it may not have hundreds of volunteer positions, its volunteers must be drawn from a smaller group of people. One pastor described such a situation in his small seventy-five-person congregation, which required forty-three volunteer slots to run the church.

Unfortunately the Faith Communities Today 2008 (FACT) research also found that conflict was more likely to occur as church size decreased. Smaller churches too were less likely to have a wide range of opportunities for service. All of the slots had to be filled to run the church—worship, choir, Sunday school, governance committees—which left little flexibility for interest-based service. Committee appointments were less likely rotated in smaller churches; lifetime appointments to a family's power slots were quite common in small churches.

Likewise we are all aware that long-term church intimacy can also turn in on itself to become isolation and inhospitable rigidity toward newer people "invading the turf." In the FACT study smaller churches were more likely to have a difficult time accepting newcomers, and no matter what size, if a church was not accepting of new people it was less likely to find volunteers easily. Conversely the survey found that the more a church was willing to change and adapt, the greater its likelihood of finding volunteers.

Size is a significant factor for involvement, but there are strengths and weaknesses at both ends of the spectrum. In essence we are suggesting that a leadership team must discover and acknowledge its natural difficulties and advantages at whatever size the church may be. Leadership must realize that the church's size will provide both opportunities and challenges for participation, and wisely craft a strategy that reflects these size-related issues.

Denominational Family

Another congregational factor that is often thought to make a difference in participation is denominational family. We want to be clear that we are not discussing theological doctrines per se (our measures did not address specific doctrinal or theological questions), although there is an implicit theological character distinct to each group.

Our point here is not to argue the theological merits of any particular denomination. Nevertheless churches from more theologically conservative denominations and faith traditions, such as Evangelicals and African American churches, had larger ratios of attenders to members than churches from mainline traditions, although that diminishes greatly when size was controlled for. Likewise this group of more conservative churches had slightly less difficulty in finding and recruiting volunteers, but this edge disappears when size, spiritual vitality, and the total number of committees were controlled for. When we control for these other factors, denominational family seems to have little influence in the participation equation, except indirectly.

The slight edge in favor of the more theologically conservative denominations should not be too surprising since they often have a higher set of participation expectations for members. In the FACT survey more-conservative churches are also more likely to be growing, have a clear vision, be open to change, have younger congregations, and enjoy a host of other factors that relate somewhat to increased participation and involvement. Together these positive factors combine to create a more conducive environment and greater expectation of involvement in the life of the gathered congregation.

We are not implying then that a stricter theological understanding of the Bible increases involvement. The surveys used did not address that question, only what denominational family the church belonged to; the relationship was quite weak when its influence was controlled by other variables. Rather factors like a sense of purpose, excitement, openness to change and accepting newcomers, higher expectations for member involvement, and a host of other variables do facilitate involvement. Generally these conditions are more likely found in churches from conservative denominations in this same study. If such factors are present in churches from mainline traditions, these churches too can be seen to draw greater percentages of participants and have less difficulty recruiting volunteers.

Worship Format and Church Dynamics

Another hotbed of dissent we want to skirt carefully is that of contemporary worship. There is only a minor positive relationship between ease of volunteer recruiting and the use of contemporary worship, as measured by having drums, electric guitars, and projection screens in worship as well as labeling the worship as "contemporary." At the same time, there is a strong correlation between these contemporary worship markers and whether a church is growing, has a sense of joyfulness and vitality, is seen as an exciting place, and is filled with a sense of God's presence.

Contemporary worship per se is only slightly related to greater participation. However, there may well be other indirect connections between modern worship forms and involvement. For instance, contemporary worship is more attractive to those under thirty-five years of age, and there is a positive relationship between ease of recruiting volunteers and having a larger percentage of younger adults in the congregation. Likewise, these worship forms correlate to growth; growing churches are marked by greater spiritual vitality, which relates to greater participation. Thus many other characteristics of a church are more likely to directly influence involvement than the worship style, as long as the worship service isn't boring, dull, and predictable.

These other characteristics of worship (beyond format, that is) and congregational life should be attended to as each is strongly related to a church's ease of recruiting volunteers

Figure 5.1 Spiritually vital churches rate highest in recruiting volunteers

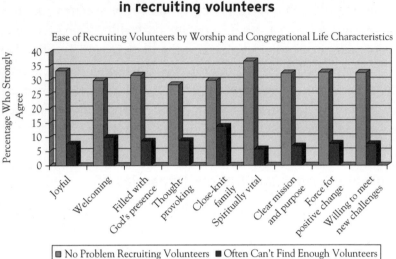

Ease of Recruiting Volunteers by Worship and Congregational Life Characteristics

■ No Problem Recruiting Volunteers ■ Often Can't Find Enough Volunteers

Source: Faith Communities Today 2008, Protestant only.

(see Figure 5.1), the percentage of people in the church actively involved in recruiting new attenders, and even (though this book isn't focused on it) rate of church growth over five years. The stronger a church rated its worship as welcoming to newcomers, joyful, filled with a sense of God's presence, and thought-provoking, the more easily able it was to recruit volunteers. Additionally, a church was more likely to recruit volunteers the more strongly it was described as spiritually vital and alive, having a clear mission and purpose, being a force for positive change in the community, and to a lesser degree like a close-knit family and willing to meet new challenges.

Likewise congregations who had an easier time recruiting volunteer leaders were more likely to describe their approach to ministry and mission along the following lines (and see Figure 5.2):

1. The church is an exciting place where people can get involved in a variety of meaningful activities.

2. The church encourages and fosters intense, intimate experiences with God.

Figure 5.2 Churches with these values have the easiest time recruiting volunteer leaders

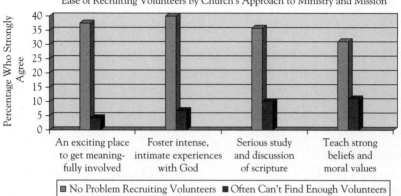

Ease of Recruiting Volunteers by Church's Approach to Ministry and Mission

Source: Faith Communities Today 2008, Protestant only.

3. People are engaged in and energized by serious study and discussion of Scripture and theology.

4. The church holds and teaches strong beliefs and moral values.

Finally those churches with less conflict, especially around money, were more likely to have easy volunteer recruitment. Thus while size and denominational tradition have mixed roles in the level of participation, the character and atmosphere within a congregation—how it is perceived—have a much greater effect on involvement. And many of these characteristics revolve around a church's spiritual attributes. Exactly how a leadership team or pastor goes about creating such attitudes in their church goes beyond the scope of this book, but it is clear that these characteristics should be goals for any leadership team wishing to increase participation.

Removing Roadblocks to Participation

If many of these spiritual and attitudinal characteristics strongly correlate with easier volunteer recruitment, what then did churches say made regular participation more difficult? The

FACT survey asked exactly that question. Of five listed options, the challenge of members being busy and overcommitted was seen as creating the most difficulty for churches (see Table 5.2). Conflicts with work schedules and with school- or sports-related activities were felt to hinder regular participation at some level for three-quarters of churches. These issues were vastly more problematic than parking, crime, or locational challenges. While there were slight variations for parking issues and crime depending on the church's location, the top two issues remained consistent across different sizes and denominational family.

This probably isn't news to anyone reading this book, but it is comforting in a misery-loves-company fashion to know that nearly all churches are suffering from this dynamic. In a sense the solution is a catch-22 for most congregations. A church can try to offer a wider array of programs with considerable flexibility to accommodate active members who struggle with time and scheduling issues. However, such expansions of offerings strain limited resources and tax the small staff and overworked volunteers that most congregations count on to do everything. Part Three, on leadership, suggests ways to address this, but it is not an easy feat, only an essential one. Such an effort is also self-rewarding since

Table 5.2 Members being busy and overcommitted is the greatest hindrance to participation

What Makes Regular Participation More Difficult?	Reported Degree of Hindrance (Percentage)			
	Not at All	A Little	Somewhat	Quite a Bit
Conflict with school- or sports-related activities	24	38	27	12
Conflict with work schedules	26	47	22	5
Driving distance to worship facility	54	31	14	2
Parking problems	64	20	11	5
Fear of crime	84	10	4	1

Source: Faith Communities Today 2008, Protestant only.

a church with a robust cadre of volunteers is more likely to be growing, be in better financial shape, and have fewer conflicts.

Care and Feeding of Volunteer Leaders

Learning what other churches do to increase volunteer participation is helpful. It is even more essential to understand from the research what positively enhances the culture of involvement and increases volunteerism.

Interestingly a quarter of Protestant churches in the FACT study reported that they had no problem recruiting volunteer leaders, while 13 percent complained they often couldn't find enough people to serve. The rest claimed that recruitment was a challenge, but they eventually find people to serve.

The FACT survey asked a battery of questions to measure the efforts churches use to address the needs of their volunteers. The picture these questions paint about what churches do offers a mixed appraisal of their efforts: some are excellent, and others need significant help. The underlying lessons in the findings, however, are crystal clear.

Less than half of the churches reported that volunteers were publicly recognized and thanked on a regular basis. And yet regular public recognition makes a significant difference. As Figure 5.3

Figure 5.3 Recognition of volunteers pays off with more success in future recruiting

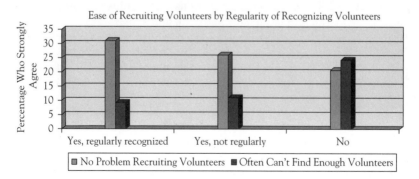

Source: Faith Communities Today 2008, Protestant only.

shows, churches that regularly recognize their involved members have fewer problems finding volunteers.

Less than a quarter of the FACT churches said they provided regular training sessions for new leaders. This goes a long way in explaining why so few congregations have no problem recruiting volunteer leaders. Yet the same survey shows that if churches engage in regular training or mentoring, they greatly decrease their problems in finding volunteers (see Table 5.3).

Likewise the more accurately the volunteers reflect the diversity of a congregation in terms of age, gender, and race, the more involved these members will be. Churches whose committees reflected the membership's diversity were four times more likely to have no problem recruiting volunteer leaders.

Further, if the church claims to do a lot of rotation of persons serving in volunteer roles, it is almost three times more likely to have no problem finding volunteers. This is a staggering statistic, and yet it points to a simple alteration in the life of a church. Rather than allowing the same people to serve or limiting the leadership rotation among a small number of folks, broaden the pool of participants by instilling term limits and caps on the number of committee roles or group leadership slots a single person can occupy at any given time. This simple change can reap great rewards in volunteer development.

**Table 5.3 The more a church trains its volunteer leaders,
the less problem it has in finding volunteers**

Levels of Training	No Problem Recruiting Volunteers	Often Can't Find Enough Volunteers
Mentoring, one-to-one training	27%	12%
Some trained, others not	17%	13%
Not usually trained	13%	18%

Source: Faith Communities Today 2008, Protestant only.

These insights taken together paint a clear picture. Any church that wants to strengthen its volunteer efforts should engage in regular training sessions and mentoring, rotate its leadership of groups, reflect its member diversity in committees, and offer public acknowledgment, reward, and recognition of volunteers. These efforts greatly reduce the challenge of finding people to serve.

If this consequence isn't enough reward, there is also a strong relationship between the ease of finding volunteer leaders and how involved members are in recruiting new people to the church, as Figure 5.4 shows. Likewise a congregation's spiritual vitality is also strongly related to the ease of finding volunteer leaders, even after controlling for size. Churches that both regularly train volunteers and give them frequent recognition are more than twice as likely to be described as spiritually vital than those that do neither.

Churches that both regularly train volunteers and give them frequent recognition are more than twice as likely to be described as spiritually vital than those that do neither.

Figure 5.4 Volunteers and inviters go hand in hand

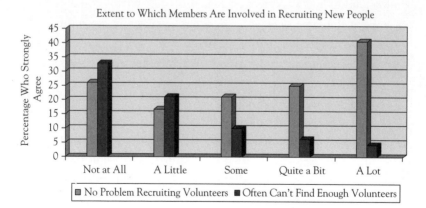

Source: Faith Communities Today 2008, Protestant only.

Committees or Ministry Activities?

Nearly all churches struggle with their members having too little time and overcrowded schedules with too little freedom to volunteer generously at church. Given that reality, church leadership must consider how to wisely expend this precious volunteer resource. An average congregation has a median of six committees or taskforces, the FACT study discovered, with most churches falling between four and nine. Mainline churches have significantly more committees than Evangelical churches.

The number of committees a church has is not directly related to increased volunteer recruitment, vitality, or growth in attendance. The inverse, not finding enough people willing to serve, is slightly related to the number of committees, especially as size decreases. Perhaps this is due in part to a lack of options or a poor division of labor within a church. It might also be tied to smaller-church dynamics, as small congregations are most likely to be in decline or have lower turnover rates for committee leaders. Clearly dynamics other than just the number of committees are at work. As one pastor described,

> I hear this a lot [the lack of broader member participation] yet our congregations are perfectly willing to have the same persons serve on several committees at the same time. I've been working hard to find ways to discourage this—like having committees meet at the same time, etc. There has been significant pushback to these efforts by certain members. I sense that control and power issues are at work here as well. In other words that seem to be saying, "We hate doing all the work, but we like to be in control of what's happening."

Those participants who are giving their all as volunteers often worry about giving less. They don't want to quit volunteering, out of love for the church, obedience to God, and a sense of duty or even out of concern that the job won't get done. As such they seldom willingly make space for others to step up to volunteer. It is like the monetary endowment that diminishes giving because everyone assumes that the church has the money it needs. An endowment of longtime volunteers (even if they are only 10–20 percent of the active members) stifles others from jumping in to help. You may hear a member comment, "All the slots are filled, and those folks have been doing it for so long, they are good at it. I wouldn't want to step on Sister Jones's toes, do her job, or take her place." But it is often also true that Sister Jones derives a sense of accomplishment, power, and prestige out of working so hard for the church. She wants help, but at the same time she doesn't really want to give up her job.

While everybody in the congregation knows that a small percentage of the attenders participate, many would like to be involved more actively. They want to use their gifts and talents, but they don't see any open positions because somebody is already filling them. And in all likelihood those folks currently doing the job would feel slighted, disempowered, and hurt if it was taken from them. Yet they would ultimately be relieved not to have to work so hard. These dysfunctional "volunteer dynamics" are not going to change on their own; they won't change without the intervention of the pastor or the intentional efforts of key lay leaders.

Considerable research suggests that when the leadership reflects the full diversity of the membership and draws on the human and social capital of all members, it is more likely to be successful. Accomplishing this can truly be a challenge. Yet as we saw above, the turnover of leadership within church committees is strongly tied to increased participation in volunteer leadership and activities. In many different ways a church must begin integrating new people, those perceived as "outsiders" (even when they have been members for decades), into the existing committees and ministry structures.

> Dysfunctional "volunteer dynamics" won't change without the intervention of the pastor or the intentional efforts of key lay leaders.

There is another question clergy should be asking themselves. If your members have only so many hours each week to contribute to the mission of the church, do you want them doing committee work or ministry? Serving on more committees will mean having little or no time to engage in ministry, worship, mission, and fellowship activities. Do you really want members to give all their energy to running the church's committees? And how fulfilling are your current committee structures and meetings for participants' spiritual lives? Is it possible to turn these organizational necessities into ministry efforts, times of worship, or spiritually infused small groups?

This again raises the question of whether committee service empowers involvement. Perhaps a shift to a more ministry-oriented service involvement would strengthen volunteerism. The FACT survey found that increasing the number of activities and programs strongly related to a church's spiritual vitality, even after controlling for the congregation's size and denominational affiliation.

Post Ushers at the "Back Door" to Follow Up on Those Who Leave?

As we have noted throughout the book, many churches have back doors as active as their front entrances. When asked, most churches say they follow up on those who leave. That is exactly what the FACT survey uncovered: 60 percent of churches reported that they would definitely contact someone who stopped attending, while only 5 percent said probably not, or only if the person was well known. This is a very optimistic portrait of the back-door hospitality teams (see Figure 5.5).

This response might well be idealistic thinking, which describes the respondents' best intentions and desires more accurately perhaps than it does their actual practice. Our experience and that of many interviewees, as well as comments on

Figure 5.5 Most churches say they would contact a lapsed member (but do they?)

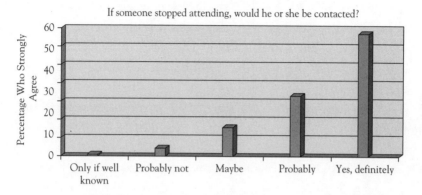

If someone stopped attending, would he or she be contacted?

Source: Faith Communities Today 2008, Protestant only.

surveys, do not bear this picture out. Listen to these stories and comments we heard during our research.

One core lay leader, Jeannine, and her husband, who were both very active in the church, got pulled away from the congregation because of his extended illness. While he was in the hospital, they were surrounded by church friends and a visit from the pastor. Then came the many months of rehabilitation and recovery, during which time they were unable to attend church. During the entire home convalescence no one from the church came to visit, connected with them, or inquired about how they were doing or when they were coming back to church. Finally, about eight months into their absence, Jeannine got a call from the church; it was someone on the "connections team" wanting to find out how they were doing. By this time Jeannine was quite disillusioned with the church's lack of concern and care; she had feelings of hurt, abandonment, and even betrayal after having served in such a dedicated and active way in the congregation. She told the connection caller that she had some issues and wanted to talk with someone from the church. And that was the last she heard from her church.

Another woman, Karen, in her late twenties, was married in her home church and, following the celebration, moved to the next state with her husband. Not a single person from the church ever connected with them about their absence until four years later, when someone from the Christian education staff called to see if she would be willing to volunteer in the children's ministry.

These comments from the parish inventories echo similar themes:

> I will have been in the area for nearly a decade—which hardly seems transient. I am not a formal member of the church, and can see how it would be easy for me to fall through the cracks. But I also think that's rather telling about gaps in how the church follows-up with its community (if not formal church) members. Again, I just want to highlight how easy it is for a once-active attendee to slip away, out of sight, out of mind, from the church community.

> The church does not care for me. It did not reach out to me when I was in need to see how I was doing. The minister never came to visit. When I did not come to church for several weeks no one asked why, so I stopped coming altogether. No one there cares about me. It has now been more than two years and not one peep from anyone at our church.

> In the eight years since I dropped away from the church, no one has ever tried to communicate and find out why, or what I am now doing.

Whether exaggerated in tone or not, the survey data do reveal that follow-up can make a difference. Contacting lapsed members is not likely to strengthen volunteer recruitment. It is, however, strongly related in our studies to more members being involved in recruiting new people. Likewise the more involved a church is with contacting visitors and following up on first-timers, the more likely it is to reach out to lapsed members too. Follow-up with absent participants is not consistently related to size, except that very large congregations (over five hundred attenders) are significantly less likely to do it. This is to be expected given their size, but they are also of a size where such a strategy is absolutely necessary. Mainline churches that were growing numerically stand out as having significantly higher levels of contact with their lapsed attenders. For more conservative denominations, contacting lapsed attenders was not directly related to increased growth of their churches. Nevertheless very high percentages of African American and Evangelical churches reported that they would definitely follow up on a lapsed person.

The Role of Clergy in Participation

We need a pastor that is ready to grow the church and take it to a new level of involvement and commitment.

Ultimately, leading the church to what the above inventory comment described as "a new level of involvement and commitment" takes a leader. There is no getting around the key position of the pastor in congregational transformation. But what effect do the pastor's actions have on facilitating the recruitment of volunteers? Or on getting members involved in recruiting others? Or on contacting lapsed members?

The clergy's characteristics made little difference in the Faith Communities Today study. Neither length of time at the church nor their age increased volunteer participation. A pastor's actions, however, made quite a bit of difference according to the FACT research. The survey asked how much time and attention clergy gave to eleven common ministerial tasks. Those clergy who focused more attention on developing and promoting a vision, evangelism, teaching about the faith, and recruiting and training lay leaders saw significantly increased volunteer recruitment.

Likewise the more a pastor devoted time to contacting inactive members, the much more likely it was for the church to reach out to lapsed persons. Additionally a pastor who spent more time focused on a congregation's vision and purpose, evangelism, and training lay leadership stood a much greater chance of the church's members being involved in recruiting new people. These same three areas of ministry were also highly correlated with high spiritual vitality.

No matter what the issue, the clergy and pastoral leadership are the linchpin. The pastor is central to why persons leave but also to how attenders envision getting the participation dynamic to change. Granted, the centrality of the pastor varies by the size of the church and the complexity of the congregation's organizational structure, yet the pastor is still the key component of change.

> The pastor is central to why persons leave but also to how attenders envision getting the participation dynamic to change.

This may be hard for a pastor to hear, but it is the perspective of many of our interviewees and comments on the inventories. While many of these persons affirmed they would willingly become involved if given the right circumstances, none suggested that they would intentionally create that circumstance at the church apart from the pastor or church leaders. In other words many folks were willing to join a small group, participate in ministry activities, or use their gifts when motivated, but they were not going to create the small-group system, start a ministry, or institute a gifts inventory program. They expected leadership to come from the church's leadership team.

> Our church is greatly in need of good pastoral leadership. The Sunday services are usually excellent but it ends there. Attendance and participation in activities and church committees as well as Sunday services is rapidly dwindling. . . .

We need growth in membership. Active participation by more members. Community involvement by more members. Ecumenical involvement by more members. Financial involvement by more members.

I want a pastor that inspires faith, promotes growth and participation of members and new members alike. I hope to see a growing church of active persons who are not the same old active group of people.

I want a pastor who can stop as many people going out the back door as are coming in the front door.

On renewing commitment and invigorating participation, the research is clear. Congregational members look to the clergy to lead, but at the same time it must be an intentional team effort of both the clergy and the laity. As one parish inventory comment stated,

Leadership has to come from the whole congregation, not just the pastor; this congregation is incredibly lazy in expecting the pastor to do everything; we need to learn to exert lay leadership.

Significant changes in participation norms and practices must come from many fronts. As Michael McMullen notes in the Faith Communities Today publication "Insights on Membership Commitment," recent organizational theory literature stresses that

Participants in an organization are more likely to be retained if they have some level of three types of commitment 1) affective commitment (emotional connections to other members of the group); 2) normative commitment (the degree to which one's own personal values and beliefs conform to organizational goals); and 3) continuance or calculative commitment which constitutes the perceived rewards for staying with or leaving an organization.

To these three our research compels us to add the dimension of spiritual commitment, whereby a person gains a sense of meaning, purpose, and spiritual fulfillment. Therefore church leadership stands a greater chance of retaining its participants and generating more robust involvement from them if it can

- Solidify emotional bonds between persons
- Communicate a clear vision of the church's ideals and give members ownership of these ideals
- Generate rewards for staying involved, such as acknowledgment, training, and leadership opportunities
- Develop in members a sense of spiritual maturity, discipleship, and spiritual fulfillment

Granted, this is no easy task, but it is a critical spiritual effort if one wants to close the back door of the church and engage the spiritual lives of all members through congregational participation. Part Three offers helpful suggestions for such a leadership task. Meanwhile, in the next chapter we address some of the latent assumptions that leadership staff often have which hinder the task of leading to greater participation.

6

MISINFORMED EFFORTS
TO BUILD PARTICIPATION

Chapter Four discussed the broader cultural influences that affect church participation, and Chapter Five explored the organizational patterns of churches that help or hinder involvement. This chapter looks at one additional influence, that of the church's own leadership approaches, especially the ones that stand in the way of participation. It could also be titled, "Mistakes Church Leadership Makes in Promoting Involvement." Leadership teams often try to encourage participation and yet in doing so miss the mark completely. At times their programs and plans actually hinder the possibility of participation for a majority of the members. Along with learning about the cultural hindrances of involvement and church structural challenges, it is often necessary for a leadership team to learn about the ways its own cherished involvement efforts can be detrimental as well.

In the previous chapter we saw that a church's new-member assimilation programs may have very little relationship to whether a church has a higher rate of volunteer activity. Active participation is really driven by other factors. Nevertheless even these initial steps with newcomers and visitors can begin to introduce them into robust participation and congregational involvement.

For example, Cynthia, a middle-age adult, was invited to her present church by a coworker who was already attending it. She had asked him a bunch of questions, so at church the following Sunday he gathered up various brochures about the church's different ministries. On Monday he handed them to her. She took them home, and also showed them to her boyfriend. Then Cynthia looked over the church website—"every page," she said. The next Sunday she and her boyfriend visited the church. "That was the quickest hour I ever sat through a service," she told us. She liked the contemporary music, and said the message "was something for me to think about, take home, and grow with."

When they came back the very next Sunday, they saw a small welcome booth that was unattended. They got some coffee from the fellowship area and then came back, but the welcome booth was still unstaffed. Cynthia walked around the area to draw attention to herself, but nobody came. While waiting, she started looking at the desk itself. She noticed a slip to fill out that offered a free gift from the church. They both filled it out and then went looking for someone to give it to. They found someone with a name tag, who they assumed to be an official volunteer or staff person. "Here are our forms," Cynthia explained. "We filled them out, and we'd like our free gift."

"Oh, I'm terribly sorry; let's go find the gift for you," the woman replied. She came back in a few minutes, unable to find the gift. She advised, "Well, write on there that you didn't get a free gift."

Cynthia, whom we met two months later, goodheartedly told us that she never did get that free gift. "Not everyone's that bold, I realize," she confessed. Even though she got less than a stellar reception and had uncertain first steps, she's been back almost every week and is now looking for what she can do next in the church.

Let's look at another example. Alvin is a young adult who describes himself as being a bit shy. When he moved away from his childhood town to a new city, he didn't look forward to finding a new church. Someone suggested that he visit a certain church, now his current church, so he checked out the church's website (an increasingly popular practice as the general public's online usage continues to grow).

The church had an "I'm new" section on its website, so he watched a video clip there. In the video a woman talked about how her faith had grown through her involvement in this church. "I was skeptical when hearing this person describe the church," he told us. "Her enthusiasm really felt a little over the top, more like a cult. So I was very suspicious." Yet he was intrigued enough to come to an actual service. At first he felt a bit overwhelmed. "I think if you've eaten cold cereal every Sunday and then you sit down in front of a T-bone steak that's kind of the shock that I experienced," he said. So he came another week. Then another.

Now what? Will he connect? What are his chances of moving into a position of involvement? How has the church helped or hindered his chances?

Cynthia and Alvin are actual people we met on our church visits. They probably represent two extremes. Cynthia is outgoing and self-initiating. Alvin is shy and cautious. In between are dozens of other kinds of people, all of whom have started attending a new church and are now ready to become more involved. In both of our cases these churches have failed—so far—to use those initial encounters to introduce these new attendees to a place of active participation.

Whatever the personality type of these newcomers, the church's leadership now has an opportunity to invite and guide them into greater engagement. An increased participation would hopefully lead them to increased spiritual growth. Ideally participation norms and expectations can be established at the beginning of new-person assimilation. Unfortunately it doesn't always happen that way.

Newcomer Involvement Patterns

It is fascinating to learn about each church's involvement model from both the staff's perspective and the newcomers' perspective. Sometimes both groups voice the same idea; other times the two groups perceive reality differently. Here are several observations we made on our church visits as we compared how people said they got involved against how church leaders say they attempt to integrate people.

1. *New people are not complete strangers: nearly all first heard about the church from friends, so someone already at the church asked them to come.* This was the case with Cynthia in the first of our two examples above. In other words most first-time guests are faintly connected in some way already. Build on that bridge.

Sometimes the connection is relational but secondhand. For example it was at her hair salon that Pat first heard about the church she now attends. The stylist didn't go to the church, but she knew a member from the church who had cancer. The hair salon worker "did nothing but rave," Pat told us, "not about the pastor but about the church itself and the support this woman was getting because she had two small children. She said you have to go to this church. She said you won't ever find a church that is so supportive."

Many churches use their website, a Facebook page, mailers, radio ads, banners on their property, or other means to invite potential visitors to a church-sponsored event. Most succeed in building awareness and helpfully so, but in the greater number of cases it's a personal recommendation like that of Pat's hair stylist where they first learn about the church and they get the hard push, or gentle coaxing, to the point of deciding, "I'm going to visit that church."

The majority of first-time guests are accompanied by the family member, friend, neighbor, or work colleague who invited them. Many others who visit alone are coming at the encouragement of a trusted personal recommendation, such as Pat's hair stylist's.

Another church where we interviewed people was near several universities. "There was a buzz at the different campus ministries that this was a good church to attend," a woman

**Table 6.1 Most people come to a church because
a person there invited them**

	How did you first find out about this church?
80%	Friend, coworker, or family member
13%	Saw church facility and came on own
7%	Media (newspaper, TV, radio, mailer, internet, etc.)

Source: Larger church survey.

named Jenny told us. She had first come to the church several decades earlier as a college student. She didn't come because she knew someone specific at the church. Rather she came anticipating that she would find people like her, some of whom she might know. That's exactly what happened.

The pathways are innumerable by which people initially find their church, but the vast majority of the time a relational factor is behind that connection (see Table 6.1). Sometimes it's overt because the guests are sitting next to the person who brought them. Other times the connection, though real, is more hidden and random, as with Pat and Jenny.

Too many pastors miss or minimize the newcomer's relational connection, which they could build on. One smaller church, where Warren was a member for many years, is typical. I appreciated the way my pastor took time in every worship service to speak to guests. He would smile, give his name, and then warmly say something like, "If this is your first time to visit us, we want to welcome you. It takes a lot of courage to come to a church *where you don't know anyone.*" He then asked them to stop by the welcome-team kiosk after the service to receive a gift bag with information on the church and a great book about the life of faith.

> Too many pastors miss or minimize the newcomer's relational connection, which they could build on.

His intentions were all great, but this approach acts as if relational connections don't matter. The oversight is rather common in the churches we observed. It's important also to train members in how to help their guests find meaningful connection points in the church's ministries. Some churches develop a "sponsor" approach designed to be a relational bridge for newcomers. Some churches intentionally overstaff their greeter stations or welcome counters so that a church volunteer can walk around with any new persons, showing the way and in the process getting to know them a bit more personally.

2. *New people are the least connected, so don't overlook the need to help them develop more meaningful relationships.* People may come to church by way of some kind of relationship, but it's often a weak connection like Jenny and the one fellow student she recognized on her first visit. They're unlikely to sit together beyond the first week (if that), much less to follow the same pathway of spiritual growth together.

If people are to feel at home in the life of a church that's new to them, they need to develop deep and meaningful relationships there. This often means forming new friends.

One of the people we interviewed in a focus group was up front about looking for friends. "My goal was to find not just a church, but a social group," he said. In another church a young man wanted a context of relationships and found them quickly. "I came by myself the first Sunday and they were pushing for community groups, which is something I knew that I needed. . . . I jumped on it and I've been going to the same one ever since."

Relational chemistry takes time and experimentation. You may meet someone at church who lives on the same street as you do, but that doesn't mean you have common interests. Likewise people may not click with each other, even if they're of the same age and life stage.

In each church we visited, we asked how people build relationships and develop new friends. Many churches have set

Table 6.2 The biggest group came to the current church from another local church

Immediately before coming to this church did you participate in another church?

44%	Yes, immediately prior I participated in a local church
28%	Yes, immediately prior I did, but I just moved into this area
18%	No, I didn't attend regularly for several years
6%	No, I had never attended anywhere
4%	No, I've been here most of my life

Source: Larger church survey.

up very intentional structures: fellowship times, socials, classes that include times of interaction, short-term service teams, and more. A few take a classroom-style approach, hoping that friendships develop "somehow" along the way. Churches like that are harder for a newcomer to break into.

New people come in with skills, talents, and interests. According to our larger church study, also confirmed by the congregational life surveys, the vast majority of new persons are not new to church life (see Table 6.2). Some of these first-timers have spent decades in church service elsewhere, and yet many churches treat them as not just new people but new Christians. Building connections also means being introduced to services, ministries, and opportunities for engagement—and intentionally trying to connect that person's natural interests and talents with what the church has to offer, as soon as possible.

3. *Churches and staff overwhelmingly see the "front door" (worship and the pastor's identity) as the way and reason folks come in,* as our research on staff's views of what attracted people to church showed. By contrast our research on what individuals themselves said (surveys and especially interviews) found that people come in through many different doors (see Table 6.3). These may include small groups, mission projects, self-help programs, and many more. And they come in for diverse reasons.

Table 6.3 Attitudes of staff and attenders clearly differ on what brings people in and what keeps them

How influential were the following in bringing you to this congregation "initially" (when you first began attending) and then in keeping you here "now"? If you are a first-time visitor, please answer only for "now."

| | What Attenders Said (1 = not at all, 5 = a lot) | | What Staff Said (1 = not at all, 5 = a lot) | |
	Initially	Now	Initially	Now
Senior pastor	3.5	4.3	4.3	4.4
Worship style	3.6	4.2	4.0	4.0
Reputation of the church	3.4	3.8	4.4	3.9
My friends and family are here	2.9	3.2	4.3	3.8
Adult programs/ministries	2.5	3.2	3.6	3.7
Children and youth programs/ ministries	2.5	2.8	3.9	4.0

Source: Larger church survey.

4. *People are more open to expanding their involvement when they're asked personally by someone they know,* so build a structure that honors relational networks. We asked the following question of about forty thousand people in larger churches: "What was the first step that moved you from spectator to active participant at this church?" To those who could remember, we offered five different responses. As Table 6.4 shows, people's answers were all over the map. Not surprisingly the lowest response was the least personal one: only 6 percent responded to an invitation from someone they did *not* know, such as at a sign-up booth or over a phone call from someone they didn't have a relationship with. The next-lowest response was also impersonal: responding to a general announcement, such as an appeal from the pulpit. A much higher response was to a personal invitation from someone they did know. The remaining two options have

Table 6.4 Attenders and staff differ considerably on how they think members get involved

What was the first step that moved you from spectator to active participant at this church?

Key Step	What Attenders Said	What Church Staff Thought People Would Say
Inward: I responded to an inward sense of call or spiritual prompting	32%	13%
Friend: I responded to a personal invitation from someone I *did* know (a friend, acquaintance, or someone on staff)	29%	56%
Self-initiative: I took initiative to look for opportunities	17%	2%
General: I responded to a general announcement (such as an appeal from the pulpit, e-mail, bulletin announcement)	16%	23%
Stranger: I responded to a personal invitation from someone I *didn't* know (sign-up booth, phone call, etc.)	6%	6%

Source: Larger church survey.

unclear relational connections: about 50 percent said they did it not relationally but rather as a self-driven effort—whether they took the initiative to look for opportunities or responded to an inward spiritual sense of call.

Other survey questions, plus our focus groups, convince us that most people take their first step toward involvement either of their own accord or in community with someone they know. By contrast too many pastors think that the pulpit, worship bulletin, or church newsletter announcement are the primary triggers for involvement. As important as such announcements are, they alone are rarely the scale-tipper. It may take some work to structure a church so that the norm is a

> Too many pastors think that the pulpit, worship bulletin, or church newsletter announcement are the primary triggers for involvement.

personal request by someone known, and the culture welcomes people taking initiative or responding to an inner prompting.

● ● ●

Neither the perceived path nor the model of integration that church leaders create really fit the way participants described their sense of how they connected or started to participate in the church. Nor do these models and paths fit the experience of the very people (the staff) who were pushing them.

People follow a cafeteria approach to involvement, so don't offer just one way. In one of our focus groups people compared their church involvement to the mix-and-match approach of a cafeteria. As one woman told us, "I worship with my husband at the 8:30 morning [service], but I'm on an evening crew of our ministry to twenty-somethings, so I usually get both sermons. And I like both services. I like the music in the evening and I like the preaching in the morning and the choir mostly."

Create and allow multiple involvement pathways to flourish. Our focus groups drew mostly people who were highly involved in the church. One of our questions asked how they had become involved. Their answers represented multiple views and messages about what the church means to different people. In short, in most churches people got involved through many different doors and at many different speeds.

By contrast when we spoke with church staff about participation dynamics, we heard a more unified and narrow view of how to become involved. The closer staff were to the senior leader, the more groupthink they displayed. *They* understood the plan, but the average member either did not or chose another way. Thus the staff is preaching one message while attenders are following a somewhat different message.

Staffs need to realize this disjunction and understand that although their cherished paths and models work, they work only for some (and probably didn't completely work even for themselves).

Again, by contrast when we spoke with church staff, most articulated a clear pathway for how someone moves from being a first-week visitor to being an involved member who is growing spiritually. In most cases staff described a linear pathway: start here, take this class next, then. . . .

The only problem is that the "great plan" didn't seem to match what the people actually did. One church had several information booths, and Warren visited all of them. At each I introduced myself to the person as a newcomer and asked how I could get involved there. They all said what I presume they had been trained to say—"You attend this class that's offered once a month"—and handed me a flyer. I thanked them, chatted a moment to change the subject, and then asked, "By the way, how did *you* get involved here?" None of these folks went to the class as their first step. Each had followed a different path: "I heard about such-and-such program" or, "A friend invited me to attend" or, "I knew someone who had been part of such-and-such ministry."

It may be helpful to learn the paths newcomers are following into participation, and to bless them. Others—including long-term, less-involved folks—might follow the same pathways.

Involvement Models

Different churches offer a variety of models for connection, but they are almost all linear, narrowing-path models. Some form of socialization and assimilation plan is absolutely essential for any church. It is important to intentionally assist someone into the life of faith, congregational fellowship, and participation.

The involvement models found in churches are a bit like the architectural layout of many church buildings. No two are exactly alike, but several common patterns emerge. Here is our sense of the more widespread approaches, offered in no particular order.

1. *Membership first.* In one church we visited, we must have asked a dozen different people, "How does someone get involved here?" and the unanimous reply was, "Join the church." So we changed the question. "Suppose we started visiting this church, brought by our friend who is on the team that makes coffee for the fellowship hour. Could we get to know some of the people here by volunteering with him?" "No, you have to join the church first," we heard. No matter how we changed the specific committee example, we received the same answer each time.

Churches like this are taking a members-only approach to involvement. Joining the church typically involves more than coming to the front of the sanctuary at the end of a service or filling out a form. There's often a class that new members must attend. It may run for many weeks. It covers doctrine and the history of the church, but it often includes gift-finding tools like a spiritual gift inventory, an overview of the church's ministries, and a strong exhortation to get involved. The thought is that you will make friends in the ministries you join. So the sequence is join the church, join a ministry, and then make friends.

2. *Newcomer classes, then options.* Other churches stretch out the first model by first offering people a get-acquainted look at the church, which does not require people to become members. Typically these classes are short term, only one or two sessions. They are optional. They expose people to the church's various ministries and invite them to appropriate groups such as a small-group Bible study or a service group ("Can you join the group that serves lunch each Thursday at the community soup kitchen?"). The newcomer class is often paired with a follow-up

membership class, at least for churches that use the idea of a formal membership. This class too helps people find ways to get involved before they commit to membership.

3. *Specific sequence.* Some churches map out a very specific pathway for involvement. Sometimes these steps are even numbered like 101, 201, 301, and so on. Typically membership comes early in the process, and each successive class leads people to a deeper commitment, in both personal spiritual disciplines and involvement. One of the first classes might be on how to develop a practice of daily devotions, how to read and learn from the Bible on your own, or how to identify your spiritual gifts and find a ministry in which to use them. Relationships develop and deepen through the different classes and the ministries they lead to.

4. *Multiple stations.* A few churches are purposely ambiguous about where to start or what to do next. These churches feel like a wedding reception where there are different food stations—cheeses here, veggie table over there, fruit smorgasbord over there—enabling a person to start at any point. They present constant opportunities for involvement in an effort to make entry-level steps as easy as possible. On any given week one-time events like a father-daughter retreat or an all-church appeal to clean up a community park are offered. There are also recurring offers such as the monthly coffee with the pastor or a new season of small groups. All have both a spiritual component and a relational component.

5. *Meetings and big events.* In this approach involvement is heavily associated with attendance at all-church settings. The idea is that people grow into maturity primarily by hearing great preaching, experiencing God in worship, and applying what they learn. The vast majority of church life centers on various churchwide services and gatherings. These are offered frequently, sometimes several nights a week. The thought is that along the way participants will meet other people and develop

relationships. As one pastor who follows this approach told us, "If we can make sure Jesus shows up regularly here, a crowd will show up as well—made up of people who need Jesus."

6. *Training and serving.* Some churches believe all involvement opportunities need to be directed beyond the walls of the church, except for the worship service and its equivalents for children and youth. The idea is that people experience their best spiritual growth by putting what they know into practice, especially through acts of service. Relationships within the church are all developed in the context of serving others, or of being trained to serve. This approach is similar to the previous one, except that it's done through service teams rather than through all-church meetings. One pastor who follows this model explained to us that after attending worship, "people need to be involved in service; take what they've learned and use it in service to others."

7. *Ultrasimplicity.* Some churches limit the options to just two or three involvement choices with the expectation that people will do all of them. These churches believe that the worship celebrations provide the instruction and vision needed, while everything else occurs in community through small groups. As Ginny from one church told us, "I've grown by always being in a Bible study, [and] I've often led them, but as long as I'm with people growing, it's really grown me at the same time." The cell-size group is the most important aspect of some churches. "If you're not in a group, you're not in the church," such churches may proclaim. In these churches every church function occurs through a group, sometimes even financial giving.

Involving Those Who Seem Uninterested

While all these newcomer models are helpful, this book isn't really about newcomers. It's about the involvement and active participation of all people, especially those we're calling the other 80 percent—those who have been associated with the church but have dropped away at some level. The newcomer material relates to these lost or wayward sheep in showing how churches try to connect people. As churches do set up systems for new people, we wonder how well those systems work for reconnecting previously involved people.

Staff must realize that few if any of these plans for newcomers address ways to build long-term participation.

In most churches the drop-off point starts within two years of attending and being a member. Reconnecting with people at this point in their involvement isn't even on the map of most orientation and participation strategies.

We need to state clearly that the dynamics that bring people in and connect them at first may well not be the same that continue to develop them and keep them involved over the long term.

> The dynamics that bring people in and connect them at first may well not be the same that continue to develop them and keep them involved over the long term.

Most of the involvement models described above could be sketched out like a funnel, opening widest at the beginning and becoming more challenging to enter over time. Further most of these funnels are tilted toward people who want to get involved, especially newcomers. Indeed new people do need help in finding their way, learning the ropes of the church, building relationships, and discovering how best to experience spiritual growth along the way. Church leaders are certainly wise and appropriate to put much energy on newcomers.

What about those we're calling the other 80 percent, the sizable group of people who identify with the church but who seem otherwise detached or perhaps only mildly interested? How do the typical involvement models affect them? In fact most of these funnels could work for the other 80 percent, though none are particularly pointed toward them. With a little creativity, however, bigger funnel openings could be made that specifically point toward those long-term members and attenders who have become disconnected or detached.

We believe the most important starting point is the way church leaders perceive the other 80 percent. The thrust of this book is to present them as a group to be valued; they should be considered part of the flock and receive spiritual care.

Here are some specific ideas:

1. *Help the other 80 percent develop relationships within the church.* Our surveys asked people what first drew them to the church, and what now keeps them there. We also asked the staff how they thought their congregation would respond. In Table 6.4 we compared the answers of both groups. The only factor the staff thought would decrease is the role of friends and family: relational factors might initially draw people to church, but they'll become less important as they return week after week. The people said differently: having "my friends and family here" increases in importance over time.

If people said the influence of "friends and family" at the church *increased* their likelihood of remaining, then it makes sense to help uninvolved people develop relationships at the church. Indeed Table 6.5 validates that approach, showing that the longer someone is at church, the more important the role of

Table 6.5 The longer you are at a church, the more important friends and family there are to you

How influential were "friends and family" in keeping you at this church "now"?

Time Going to This Church	Importance on Scale of 1 (Low) to 5 (High)
Less than one year	2.9
1–2 years	3.0
3–5 years	3.1
6–10 years	3.3
More than 10 years	3.6

Source: Larger church survey.

friends and family is in keeping them there. Thus one approach for helping people raise their participation level is to assist them in developing greater friendships in the church.

2. *Remember that relational frameworks help people not to lose heart or drop out.* We were touched by the candid statement made by Simon, a six-year member in one of our focus groups. He spoke highly of the preaching and the worship. Then he said: "My small group [has been] a massive part of my spiritual growth and service. . . . To be honest, I don't think I've actually grown that much in recent years, but being in a small group and in some sort of service keeps me in there until, God willing, I find some more momentum." His small group and service area are "keeping me alive," he said; through them, "I'm seeing a new spurt of spiritual vigor."

Simon's story, as that of others, affirms that relational frameworks are essential for people to stay connected, involved, and growing. Through all of these connections people see God at work. As one couple told us, "What is keeping us here and what has got us fired up is just the fact that we feel that, you know, God is here, God is doing stuff, [and] the vision that is being cast . . . has appealed to us significantly." People like that are usually there for the long haul, but we suspect that all their perceptions of God at work are in a context of God working through *people*.

3. *Try small groups as a connecting point.* We asked church staff what they view as the greatest source of spiritual growth for people. We offered ten different options. Table 6.6 shows what staff think, selecting one choice far more than the others—small groups that have a spiritual orientation. A natural bridge then is for involved people to invite less-involved people to a group that they're part of.

Think about what was learned in Chapter Four about the culture we live in. Think too about previous material in this book on what impulses led to greater participation: we found a lot of individualism, attention to personal needs, and diverse

Table 6.6 Group life is thought by staff to be the greatest point of spiritual growth

Source of greatest spiritual growth for people at the church

Prayer, spiritual discussion, or Bible study groups	37%
Teaching in church's main gatherings	18%
Worship in church's main gatherings	11%
Sunday school or church school	11%
Service in ministries beyond the walls of the church	8%
Other small-group activities	5%
Service in ministries within the walls of the church	4%
Fellowships, clubs, or other social groups	4%
Support or recovery groups	3%
Community service or social justice groups	1%

Note: Only one choice was allowed.
Source: Larger church staff survey.

interests. How can you have everyone walk a path to involvement but also make that path infinitely variable to individuals' needs?

Perhaps employ several models, making them customizable to individuals. If you use only one model, then you are going to connect with only a percentage of the people. In the FACT study it was not which assimilation approach one used that made a difference in church growth or member recruitment but how many. The more approaches you use, the greater your chances of incorporating people.

> The more approaches you use, the greater your chances of incorporating people.

The ideal approach is more like a river flowing into a broader delta rather than a wide river being forced into a narrow channel. Yet how many of our cherished staff models, including those above, work toward conformity rather than the discovery of unique gifts and planting people in whatever location they might flourish.

The disjunction between staff/leadership models of participation and what individuals want and need is most clearly seen
in our questions of what moved members to active participation.
We have discussed this previously for members' responses, but
we also asked church leadership the same question: What did
they think moved members to participation? (See Table 6.4.)

Most important, staff grossly underes-
timated, underperceived, and underval-
ued the individual's personal initiative
in becoming involved, whether self-
motivated or spiritually motivated,
this being chosen by nearly 50 percent
of member respondents versus only 15
percent of staff respondents.

> Staff grossly
> underestimated,
> underperceived, and
> undervalued the
> individual's personal
> initiative in becoming
> involved.

There were other wide differences
between the people and church staff.
The staff doubled the importance of
the relational component (being asked
by a known person) compared to the people: roughly 30 percent
of members compared to roughly 60 percent of staff selected this
option. Staff think this component is important perhaps because
they are people persons, they stress relationships and relational
evangelism, and they train teams to do this. Plus their church
programs emphasize the same.

Staff also emphasized church initiatives like general announcements and bulletins since this was their work, their mode. Their
ratings were 7 to 8 percent higher than attenders'. Yet as one of
our opening stories highlighted, the motive of personal initiative
is present regularly.

Making the Effort to Bring Them Back

We loved the comment of one leader we interviewed: "God's
not going to send us more people than we can care for, so
we've got to be ready," she said. This was a church that puts

a huge emphasis on people learning to reproduce their roles and their ministries through others. They do a great job of it, in fact. As she told us, "I've almost always had an apprentice leader in everything I do," and so have most other lay leaders at the church.

At this church most ministry and spiritual formation occurs through small groups. "Small groups are really important [here]," said this leader. "That's really how you get to know people."

But certainly not everyone has made this discovery. One couple had been at this church for ten years, but the husband had never been in a small group. One small group had many people in it who knew this man, so they often prayed for him by name. Several of them invited him to be part of their group— or any group, for that matter. And they weren't alone in reaching out to him. Over time his wife and others in the church alerted him to various opportunities that could help him move from the margins toward greater participation and connection with the church.

He finally decided on his own to become more involved in the church, in his case making the bridge through that persistent small group. He came, and he loved it. "Once you're in a small group, you realize how good they are," our interviewed leader explained. "Those are your real friends. You do life with your small group. Those are the people you can call in the middle of the night."

Here was one more wayward sheep brought back into the fold. He came through one of many possible pathways at this church, by a relational bridge and by a choice that he made. This person discovered along the way how rewarding it was, both spiritually and relationally, to participate more actively.

7

HOW TO CREATE A LEARNING TEAM

"Why doesn't anyone want to volunteer anymore?" We heard this from a pastor today as we were working on this chapter. He's been in ministry about twenty years, and he went on to lament that the old ways of getting people involved don't work anymore. "It's like I have to figure out another language that will connect with them," he said.

Perhaps he does. He doesn't need to relearn English, but we suspect he does need to be schooled in how the culture has changed, especially in his community, and how that impacts the way people approach involvement at his church.

When we asked him how people do volunteer at present, he explained that patterns of church participation are all over the map. Some people give money but not their time or talents. Some volunteer enthusiastically but don't agree with much of what the church teaches. Some show up for every worship service, group meeting, or event but never invite a friend to one. To add to the confusion, a small but growing number of people call more than one place their "church home" or locate their membership in more than one congregation. Does that mean they now have two places and are not involved in either?

The Who and the What

This chapter invites church leaders to form a "Learning Team." Whatever name you use for it, the goal is to uncover the external social and cultural dynamics in your community that may indirectly hamper church involvement. In other words this team will look for patterns of behavior in the larger society that impact member participation. It may cover individual issues that could be addressed, collective patterns that could be changed, new social programs that could be instituted through your church, or larger spiritual issues that could be tackled.

> The goal is to uncover the external social and cultural dynamics in your community that may indirectly hamper church involvement.

This is the second (and final) short-term team this book recommends that your church create. The first was a Listening Team, outlined in Chapter Three. We asked you to reach out, as personally as possible, to everyone associated with your church in any way. We provided five different involvement categories, taken from Chapters One and Two, for assessing each person's involvement level. We then suggested specific actions the Listening Team might take after its round of interviews or surveys is complete.

Persons who are asked to join a Learning Team should include members who are thrilled by research, who enjoy exploring social dynamics, or who are well connected in the community. Even more important they must also be recognized influencers in the church, that is, people in a position to implement what is learned. The quickest path to a frustrated effort is to ask a group to learn and dream, but not to empower it to act. Too often if they merely report back to another group, such as a board, the energy and creative ideas die a painful death. If it was optional to have a pastor on the Listening Team, the Learning Team will need at least one person in leadership with authority to act. Having one or more recognized leaders also sets an appropriate stage if the Learning Team discovers how the church structure or management style needs to be modified.

What to Do

Our recommendation is that the Learning Team follow a parallel path with the Listening Team. First review Chapters Four, Five, and Six and narrow down a tentative list of five or so specific areas for the Learning Team to explore.

Then perhaps hold one or two meetings with the Listening Team. Affirm that you do not want them to break any confidentialities. Tell them your task and then ask to listen to and learn from them. Here are some specific questions you might ask the Listening Team:

1. Without revealing any names, could you tell us some of the *individual* reasons that you heard for (a) lack of involvement, (b) diminishing involvement, and (c) increased and robust participation? We'd love to hear personal dynamics, stories of what worked and what didn't work, and your sense of opportunities and hindrances.

2. Would you help us to think about patterns that you heard most frequently, such as across the individual stories? What were the paths that facilitated involvement, or the barriers that kept many out? Which back doors became the most common avenues of exit?

3. What do you see as the biggest needed fixes to the congregational system, which once communicated adequately could remedy a number of the individual (personal) issues? For instance would better use of the congregational database and a visitation team solve the disconnection a number of the homebound members feel? Or would changes to the church website help people keep in touch better? Maybe you heard praise for our welcoming or hospitality team but also heard a need for a care-giving team to address the needs of the long-term members in the congregation. As you heard from people about prayer, visitation, accountability,

and more, did you sense that these are all individual, personal issues, or are larger fixes needed?

4. Would you please comment on the areas the Learning Team might explore? Do you have advice or additional ideas for areas to learn about? (For example if one of the Listening Team's conclusions was that people did not feel communicated to very well, that team might advise your team to learn about how other organizations—the growing church across town, the volunteer fire department that's a major player in your community, or the local public library that seems to have a huge network of volunteers—are communicating with their people.)

Now the Learning Team can refine its task and move from preliminary research topics to more focused ones. Try to settle on a manageable number of problems to address, perhaps five at most. Agree on a time frame for the research, reminding one another that you want to do more than understand the larger dynamics that affect church participation. Rather you want to land on realistic and specific action points that will remove barriers to involvement.

A good starting point is to get a sense of community dynamics affecting the lives of congregational members.

If you need a starting point, the team might look at census data (starting with the "American Factfinder" link at www.census.gov) to see the normative family structure, average commute times, percentage of the community that moved each decade, home ownership, and other influential factors. Likewise town or city planning reports often describe growth and mobility factors, as do realty and chamber of commerce websites. You can find amazing resources through a few hours of using www.google.com with search words like "[your town/city name] growth and planning."

If these efforts of the Learning Team seem disconnected from the task of assessing your membership's individual motivations for participation, remember that community dynamics have an influence on everyone in the area, including your members. These dynamics may include patterns of civic engagement, sports schedules, overall mobility of the population, and even the hours of grocery stores and malls.

Your team might also want to interview a few civic leaders to see whether secular clubs and civic groups exhibit participation patterns similar to what the church is experiencing, or whether there are lessons to be learned from these secular organizations.

Finally the Learning Team might want to map the religious ecology (easily done in Google Maps: first map your congregation's address, then "search nearby" for "churches"), not necessarily to identify the competition but to see if collaborative church partnerships might be discovered. In this day, when nearly 70 percent of churches have websites, it is a simple task to search for like-minded local churches willing to share in joint ministries. A simple web search can generate a list of existing programs and services in other congregations that your members might plug into as volunteers, or avail themselves of, if your church cannot provide such ministries.

Making Your Findings Specific and Actionable

Review what your Listening Team discovered. You may well have identified a long list. In the overall congregational dynamics, what patterns did both teams discern collectively? Were there many stories of pastoral inattention to needs, or a lack of places to volunteer, minister, and be engaged? Did you learn about a need for training or for leadership development? Are all the "slots" in your church filled, revealing the need for more and different places to be involved, for gifts assessment, for creative use of partnerships, or for mentoring programs to give more people leadership opportunities?

Were there indications of deeper, ingrained difficulties that are diminishing involvement? Were there personality patterns that go beyond individual disagreements? You might have learned of a lack of spiritual leadership or a dynamic of turf-guarding. You might have found conflicts and significant emotional or trust wounds that need resolution or repair.

Diminished participation involves more than personal issues. It also stems from systematic issues that have potentially programmatic remedies. Within that realm the ideas from the Learning Team might have a number of different applications.

> Diminished participation involves more than personal issues. It also stems from systematic issues that have potentially programmatic remedies.

Maybe the Learning Team needs to talk further with someone in the community. Perhaps you learned that Sunday-morning sports schedules are keeping youth, and thus their parents, away from church. Given these potential conflicts, and knowing that parents today often choose their children's athletic development over their spiritual nurturance, perhaps various leaders in the church (especially parents who have children in those leagues) could hold conversations with league officials and ask whether they would be willing to shift practice times or explore other creative alternatives to scheduling games during church times.

Another strategy might be to change something your church does. As a way of accommodating today's changing culture of long work commutes, some churches are concentrating their weeknight family-related programming into one night and combining it with a meal. This way, harried parents get a good meal for the whole family, relationship-building fellowship, and wholesome activities that offer spiritual nurture to them and their children.

Still another approach might be to create something new for your church that responds to the surrounding culture. As Halloween approaches, for instance, people are reminded that they don't know their neighbors like they used to. They're also increasingly wary of sexual predators and tainted candy. In response some churches are creating Harvest Festivals, both for their own children and as an outreach to the neighborhood. Kids can still dress up and get candy, but they're no longer wandering from house to house in neighborhoods they don't know. Some parents want to avoid anything related to the demonic (costumes or activities about witches, devils, and so on); the Harvest Festival approach can encompass that goal as well.

One further idea might be to partner with existing programs in your community. Suppose your research found that the biggest area of increased involvement in your community is in serving those in need of food. Suppose your church doesn't do much service in the community. Finally suppose your team's review of local health and social service agencies found a thriving Meals on Wheels or a charity that delivers groceries. Maybe your church could strategize about recommending these places of service for members inclined to social service.

Together both the Listening and Learning Teams may have come up with many great ideas. The next step is to prioritize them. Keep in mind that the goal is to remove barriers to participation. Which ideas are most strategic for helping people become more involved with the church, ideally in a way that will assist their spiritual development?

Dealing with Leadership Challenges

If the Listening Team's evaluation of individual participation was difficult, the Learning Team's evaluation may be harder when it looks at larger issues. Some of its learnings may raise the need to address collective flaws and possibly destructive patterns within the congregational leadership or church programs. Such obstacles can be very challenging to acknowledge honestly. It is a task that must be approached prayerfully and with spiritual humility. A single squeaky wheel may be overlooked, but evidence of faulty maintenance of the congregational engine or, worse, a broken and nonfunctional vehicle must be addressed, no matter the cost or pain.

The next part of this book is entitled "Leading" because we are certain that good leadership is essential in order to finish the journey of increasing the participation and involvement of "the other 80 percent." Some of the steps may be painful, some hard, and some very fulfilling. The desired outcome is greater engagement and greater spiritual growth. As those things happen, there will be much joy, and the journey will be seen as worthwhile, both to start and to continue.

Part Three

LEADING

No matter how many green pastures and still waters a church offers to first-timers, if the tenured sheep end up with the worn-out fields and the same old muddy brooks, the congregation will never mature spiritually.

Spiritual leadership of the congregational flock includes good information gathering. The right knowledge is power, and in this case it is the power to address the unspoken needs and desires of church members to commit to their church and to a fulfilling and exciting life of faith. Listening to the congregation, as individuals, is where it begins. By now you know that this doesn't mean talking just to your heavy-duty, superengaged participants. You also want to know about those who seldom show up, those we call the other 80 percent. But this also may entail learning about the church and community structures that hinder that 80 percent from connecting.

You want to use all this information to identify relevant steps to take in leading back those who have wandered off. In addition this knowledge will aid you in your strategy of balancing the care of seasoned members with an energetic appeal to newcomers.

Leadership in an informed manner means knowing your people and seeking God's will for them. Leadership with wisdom requires knowledge combined with a spiritual sensitivity to what God wants for your particular flock.

The final part of this book shows a church leadership team how to put the previous chapters into practice. Chapter Eight begins with suggestions of small steps to improve and expand on what you already do well. Chapter Nine offers bolder strategies for how to broaden participation and woo marginal members into more dynamic involvement. Chapter Ten brings us back to what's really at stake: the ultimate endeavor for a congregation's leaders isn't church growth, member involvement, or even full attendance at worship services so much as the spiritual development and vitality of all the members of your flock.

8

START WITH WHAT YOU DO WELL

I (Warren) remember a certain board meeting at a church where I was an elder. I had asked for permission to phone all the households that were new to the church in the last two years. In my round of calls I asked everyone the same question: "What ministry helped you most in connecting with the church, bringing you to a point of involvement where you felt the church had become 'your' church?"

The top three answers accounted for almost all the people I interviewed (all were adults). They were the quarterly women's seminar, the youth group, which involved parents in various ways, and the weekday nursery school, which likewise did a lot of activities with the parents. I reported this to the board, suggesting that if that is what God is blessing, then we should put greater emphasis on these ministries. This might involve praying more for them, making public heroes of them as role models, increasing their budgets, and touching base with the leaders more regularly to make sure they feel cared for and have the resources they need.

Unfortunately no one jumped on my recommendation as the brilliant breakthrough I thought it was. The pastor at the time was a rather passive leader, and he was characteristically complacent. The long-standing treasurer commented that the current budget was fixed, and there wouldn't be any money to make changes next year either. Another person said something I didn't understand, words to the effect that we need ministries for existing members as well. He mentioned one much loved family who had dropped away from our church. After a pause in which no one commented further, the discussion moved to the next item on the agenda.

I went home frustrated that night, but I've pondered that experience from time to time. Working on this book, I think I finally understand what happened. I still feel the pastor needed to show leadership, even if just to say something encouraging in response. He could have steered the conversation toward some kind of action we could take. More important, I realize now that the members of our church board were all longtime members. They were glad we had ways for newcomers to become involved, but they were also lamenting the fact that we perhaps weren't doing likewise with the people this book is calling the other 80 percent. The folks in that group, including the family that had faded away, were their friends. As we point out in the opening to Part Three, it is critical to balance energetic appeals to newcomers with care of existing members.

> It is critical to balance energetic appeal to newcomers with care of existing members.

If I were doing that same project today, I'd propose calling two lists. I would again phone newcomers, but I would also contact a number of the church's more marginal members. I would ask this latter group a parallel question: "What ministry of the church, past or present, has helped you most to feel that this church has become 'your' church?"

Then in my report back to the board I'd help them know what to concentrate on, both for newcomers and for those who were on the church's edges. Our church had a lot of good things going for it, but it lacked certain intentionality. Our "one size fits all" mentality overlooked valuable perspectives on how to build on existing momentum.

Start with Prayer

Part One of this book was about *listening* to those who attend but are uninvolved. Part Two showed you how to *learn* from ways the broader culture is shaping people. Are you to the point of identifying the ways your church clearly addresses their spoken needs and desires? If so, in Part Three we ask how you can improve your *leadership* efforts to do so. In the process we suspect you will increase the participation of "the other 80 percent," but also you'll make church life more meaningful for all your members.

Don't start by looking for a magic spice guaranteed to make every dish tastier. No matter what "magic spice" advertisements for church-related seminars may promise, participation levels at church do not change simply by applying a new technique. The change process entails discerning spiritually how best to address the needs of your flock in order to encourage their involvement and spiritual growth. This effort should be steeped in prayer, Scripture, and faithful discussion with the entire leadership team. Thus the church's leadership should start this discernment process in a retreat or through an extended period of spiritual exploration. Through prayer and spiritual searching the leadership team should prepare for the journey the church is about to take, and should seek the direction in which God would have the congregation go. This goal is a spiritual one, that of increasing and deepening faithful participation in the congregation and an active life of faith. Therefore the process must also be spiritual and not just a mechanical application of ideas with the idolatrous goals of producing greater numbers to pack the sanctuary, generating more dollars to balance the budget, or making the task of filling committee slots easier on the pastor.

Discerning God's will and creating unanimity of purpose among the church's leadership group must happen before moving forward. This is a visioning task that uses data collection and evaluation to strategically plot a spiritual venture. When the clergy, staff, and lay leadership are of one mind and spiritually convinced that this effort is a worthy and faithful direction for the church, only then are you ready to move forward.

Proceed with Your Best Efforts

A good first step is to begin where you are. Begin reaching out to your marginal participants by assessing, strengthening, and improving—essentially doing more and better of—whatever you are doing that already promotes participation. Perhaps those are the avenues that God is already blessing?

> Begin reaching out to your marginal participants by doing more of whatever you are doing that already promotes participation.

Every congregation has highly committed, heavily involved, and actively participating members. Why are these shining, happy people so involved and engaged in certain church groups and ministries? Beginning with your strengths is as good a place to start improving participation as any. What are you doing right? Which facets of your church generate the most enthusiasm? Which groups, ministries, programs, or heaven forbid, committees are easiest to recruit for? Is the choir always overflowing? Does the altar guild continually have to turn people away? Do the monthly potluck dinners extend long into the evening and stimulate positive comments for weeks afterward? Is the Tuesday evening men's golf ministry constantly attracting too many foursomes to fit the time slots?

Look for those positive facets of your congregation that seem naturally to elicit abundant participation. Try to figure out what it is about these venues that works. What causes them to excel? Can these successes be further strengthened or duplicated? In other words can you expand on what is already working? But more importantly what lessons can be learned from these successes and applied to less-involved volunteer endeavors?

While you are examining your programs, ask existing volunteers if in fact they are involved, happy, and growing spiritually. Do some of your church's most active participants serve out of obligation and duty but would indeed like to be doing more meaningful and interesting activities? Serving on a committee that continually squabbles over liturgical colors or underfunded mission efforts is seldom enjoyable for anyone except lawyers and conflict resolution consultants.

Likewise as you capitalize on your strengths, ask yourself, "What ministries and activities may not be working well for anyone in our church, much less for our marginal members?" The answer to this question will point you to certain efforts that should be discontinued, and projects and committees that ought to be put to rest. If you decide to keep them, then where do the difficulties lie? Is it that no one is interested? Is it the membership's lack of personal spiritual motivation, or is it something that has outlived its relevance but not its slot on the organizational chart? Does the denomination mandate an elaborate structure that members are unwilling to support because they have become disillusioned by pronouncements from your denomination's national office? Do some of the challenges rest with an aging population that is plagued with illness, transportation difficulties, and safety concerns? Or is the church in competition with households facing school and sports demands and long-distance commutes that impinge on the few hours left for family or personal time?

Affirm Your Expectations for Commitment

The next step is to take stock of current congregational ideals around participation. What is currently being taught about participation and then modeled at your church?

Imagine everyone who has been at your church five or more years receiving a letter asking anyone who is not involved to resign, leave the church, and find another church. Earlier we cited examples of actual churches that did just that through their teaching. If such a sermon or letter were voiced at your church, how many people would express surprise that you expect every follower of Christ to be involved with Christ's body—the church?

What messages are the leadership, the sermons, the education classes, and the culture of the church proclaiming about what it takes to be a "good Christian" in this church? Week after week your congregation picks up overt ideas as well as unspoken practices related to Christian involvement. These become the functioning norms for participation at your church. For those who consider themselves members (or whatever word you use for church-based discipleship), what would they describe as the church's expectations for worship, spiritual disciplines, and service in Jesus' name to the community around your church? How often are members asked to give financially, and at what level? Is stewardship seen as giving one's time, talents, and income? If so, do programs and ministries allow for the exchange of this expanded sense of social capital? Do the worship service bulletins, the website, and pulpit announcements remind people that everyone is expected to be involved?

As the leadership begins to evaluate the spoken and enacted ideals currently conveyed, remember some of the lessons of Chapter Four. Language usage has changed, and the meaning of terms like *volunteer* or *member* implies radically different things to different generations. Chapter Four also signaled a shift toward a less religion-literate American population that may need to be schooled on the most basic Christian values and norms. Do you teach basic norms and values to all your adults, or just to youth and new members? Or do you assume they know already or will pick up these ideas? Additionally the increasing level of switching between religious groups and denominations may mean that few of your members carry around the spiritual toolkit that many church leaders take for granted as something everyone brings from their cradle years in church.

If you find your explicit or implicit expectations for Christian participation in your congregation to be lacking, a simple response is to raise the commitment bar. Perhaps it's just being more clear by regularly voicing what it means to be both a Christian and a participant in your congregation. Certainly this is easier said than done. But if it isn't ever attempted, the link between higher participation and an optimal Christian walk will never happen. This isn't to say that congregational participation won't increase, but remember that the goal is spiritual growth and development, not just involvement. One can hit a distant target with an arrow by raising the angle of the shot, but it may also be possible to hit it by applying more force. It is just easier to aim higher. Our experience and considerable research have shown that those congregations with higher commitment ideals do in fact experience greater levels of commitment.

Such changes in expectations need not be heavy-handed; they can be introduced gradually, gently, and compassionately—but also with spiritual passion and values that draw from the teachings of Scripture. The congregation can be inspired through other members' stories and challenged by the model of exemplary friends. The activities and narratives of the church can shift to increasingly promote the idea that God expects great things from the congregation, both individually and collectively. Leadership should preach and teach the ideal but at the same time accept people's level of participation wherever they are at the moment. The goal is increased involvement, not increased guilt.

It is a challenging feat to raise congregational expectations generally without creating animosity between the already highly committed members and those less-motivated members. You can

> The goal is increased involvement not increased guilt.

overcome this in part by enlisting some of the most committed to act as examples, to give their testimonies, and to tell their stories. You can highlight those excelling in participation, and not just those who give a lot. Strengthen and reinforce each dimension of participation separately. Think of the New

Testament metaphor of the body: some hands do missions; some brains serve on committees; some feet perform service; some stomachs cook great church suppers. Make the multiple options for excellence in participation apparent by acknowledging those who are already engaged in the roles.

Above all communicate the message of higher expectations to everyone; don't just "preach to the choir." If you use only the worship service to emphasize the new norms, how will the less involved hear? Consider those folks who come once or twice a month: they will get the message only if it is mentioned every week—although then the weekly regulars might feel preached at and perhaps get resentful. And what of those who very seldom come: how will they get the message? Consider other ways then to propagate the message to those who don't show up for worship. Use the newsletter, direct mail, e-mail, and even personal visits to persuade your inactive people that God asks more of believers than a once yearly checkup. Their mental image of the church they are not attending is the only one they know. You can't convince them that the church is changing unless they get the word directly.

Reevaluate the Process of Participating

If expectations are raised, so too your existing places for service and involvement must be examined, evaluated, and perhaps improved. You don't want to preach that Jesus is the bread of life and increase your members' longing for bread only to offer them a stone. The last thing you want is to invigorate members to serve and then have them find that all positions for service are already taken. Guarantee that the church will have places for involvement in ministry and service open and available. Make sure your current ministries, committees, and ways of involvement are as inviting and "user friendly" as possible. This may require you to bring a higher level of professionalization to current roles and tasks. This can be as simple as creating lists of service and participation opportunities, clarifying the duties of these roles, making sure you have term limits, and rotating leadership as necessary. You might also want to establish a monitoring system that periodically evaluates participation opportunities, solicits feedback from those involved, asks for improvement suggestions, and sensitively evaluates a ministry's functions and leadership. Remember, the goal is increased involvement of all, not the creation of fiefdoms and cliques that stroke the egos of a few.

Examine the range of ways people can participate in the life of the congregation in addition to worship services. Do your current "volunteer slots," those predefined places to serve, actually exclude portions of your membership? They might if you don't think it through. New parents often need childcare. Older retirees might need daytime opportunities to serve or require help with transportation. If most of your existing ministries require a year-long commitment, perhaps design onetime or limited-time opportunities to serve that will appeal to different tastes, interests, and levels of availability.

Are you also equipping those who are currently serving? What level of training, orientation, or mentoring are you providing? This is essential, not only for teachers, vestry or board members, and office volunteers but also for greeters, nursery workers, lawn caregivers, and parking lot attendants. Ask

> The goal is increased involvement of all, not the creation of fiefdoms and cliques that stroke the egos of a few.

yourself what participants need to know to do the job well and whether the church is giving them that information. Use your own knowledgeable people; establish a training or mentoring system whereby those who have the gifts and skills instruct those who don't.

If your congregation has never trained the persons who are serving, develop ways to train both those new to service and also the longtime volunteers. Plenty of seminars are available, both online and in person, on every dimension of congregational life, from church hospitality to youth ministry. Assign one person in every activity the duty of keeping current on new ideas. And draw on the skills and expertise of the congregation. Elementary education teachers of special needs children might not want to serve in the Sunday school class that targets those children in your church, but they could be ideal for offering training to those who are leading that class.

Help People Use Their Gifts and Interests

Much has been written about the need to identify the gifts and strengths of congregational members and then to help match them with suitable ministries to try. Offering the membership a gifts assessment, strengths identification, and talents inventory is indeed a good beginning. Many online options exist, both free and for a fee. However, offering a means for people to identify their gifts is again only a mechanical solution unless you cultivate the spiritual underpinning that is the internal motivation to act on the findings of an inventory.

The survey findings we reported earlier did not show a correlation between *identifying* gifts and participation, but they did show a relationship between "church leaders helping you *find and use* your gifts and talents" and involvement. Remember, the vast majority of participants in the twenty-five larger churches we studied traveled paths that were marked by internal motivation more than external requests from friends or anonymous calls for service. Motivation is created by inspiring, envisioning, and leading. It comes as a result of hearing and seeing the examples of others and having models that exemplify a life of service and involvement. You can also get members to reflect on a "purpose" and an individual sense of calling. Their talents need to be identified, and they need to begin to think about the expression of those talents through involvement as a Christian. Participation should tie their interests and passions with the needs and activities of the church. This moves volunteering past "slot filling" and toward service that builds people's spiritual lives; as Alban Institute consultant Larry Peers comments, it is "volunteering that has a soul."

As we visited vibrant churches of many sizes, we saw ample evidence of such participation opportunities. We saw congregational musicians happily teaching their craft to elementary kids who were struggling to learn their newly acquired first instrument. We watched beauticians giving their time and talent in offering free haircuts and styles to out-of-work community members. We interviewed nurses who provided foot care for the homeless, and mechanics who repaired donated cars for low-income families.

There are ministries that help people live out the call of God; many are initiated by the people in a church. They could include tutoring, flower planting, arranging altar cloths, vacuuming, reading Scripture aloud, and serving on the finance committee.

Ideally the involvement creates fulfillment, joy, and enthusiasm for the participants. In this day and age, service to God through one's church need not be drudgery or soulless work. As we noted in Chapter Four, today's culture induces us to look for and find fulfillment in our activities. Perhaps previous generations found value in sacrifice and service out of obligation, but that is less likely today. Greater time-constraints and competing interests create hard choices between church involvement and work, family, or leisure opportunities. Today the activities of a life of faith must bring intrinsic rewards, including contentment, passion, and spiritual satisfaction. In essence one's participation at church should be at least as fulfilling, if not more so, than the alternatives of a relaxing morning with a bagel and newspaper, attendance at a child's little league game, or a recreational outing with one's spouse. If the spiritual activities don't measure up with these and hundreds of other activities competing for the average American's time, then folks may well remain in "the other 80 percent."

Individualize Avenues of Participation

We often hear laments about rampant individualism in our society. Indeed there is much to bemoan about how this cultural reality shapes the church. However, if this is the current reality, then shouldn't churches acknowledge and in part embrace it in their strategies? We should assume that members come preconditioned by the society to long for a spiritual path that fits their individual interests and personal needs. Americans expect everything they "consume" will be tailored to their desires, providing flexibility and choice. However, church leadership must also strive to move members past contemporary cultural norms and social values to nurture a Christian culture that is distinctive from the surrounding secular options.

A congregation that can provide an "individualized experience" creates a resonance with the internal and often unspoken desires of the participant. Such an approach doesn't mean you have to reinvent your congregation. Think about diverse ways to address these individualized interests and personalized paths with your existing offerings. Essentially it means envisioning your ministries, programs, educational offerings, and service activities as a college catalog or a cafeteria-style buffet. If a church assumes that all participants should involve themselves in spiritual activities, receive continual education, engage in small-group settings, serve the larger community, and lead or train for leadership, then consider these categories your broad college requirements or menu groupings. List all possible offerings under each of these categories, much as a college might say that you need two science credits, three English credits, and so on. This approach ensures a balanced coverage of all key components of a faithful life without specifying a set path. It allows personalized options and choice.

If such an approach is adopted, then some manner of account-ability can be created, much like a guidance counselor in school. Several churches we have studied have simply assigned spiritual mentors or something less formal—think of the old camp model of "swim bud-dies" who hold each other account-able for selecting and following the path they choose through the options provided.

> It means envisioning your ministries, programs, educational offerings, and service activities as a college catalog or a cafeteria style buffet.

One church we visited even went as far as creating a form for these two-person teams to use, calling it a personalized "flight plan." It allowed an amazing way to personalize, even custom-ize, an individual's spiritual journey. When tied to a supportive coach and embedded in a small-group structure, it embraced diversity with accountability.

Such customized plans resonate with nearly every sphere of our daily lives. No one tells us what to eat or read, how to navigate through the stores in a shopping mall, when to exercise, what time we must watch our favorite shows (thanks to internet archives, Hulu, Netflix streaming movies, and on-demand cable television viewing). Nor do we have set national hours to engage our friends by e-mail, Facebook, texting, or phone conversations. How many of us have taken a predawn airplane flight, amazed that the person next to us in the airport terminal is texting or talking away with someone who is also awake!

More and more of life is asynchronous, built around our individualized time frames. And this freedom of choice should include everyone, not just adults. Involvement, service, educa-tion, and ministry are part of a person's faith at any age. There-fore invite everyone to be engaged in the life of the church in ways that appeal to each age group.

We saw one large congregation in Minnesota dramatically involve children in the worship life of the church. The older elementary children, just beginning to acquire skills with singing, musical instruments, and audio/video components, were guided by adults to deliver a simplified worship service for the younger children. These four-to-seven-year-olds were enraptured watching the "big kids" lead worship, while the older children beamed with pride and professionalism, as they did a very competent job with announcements, choruses and music, PowerPoint background images, and art.

Moving down the hall, we found a group of high school kids leading supervised worship for the middle schoolers. Then for the majority of high schoolers, worship was led by college-age and other young adults. This model created considerable participation and development of skills in the younger members as it formed leaders who would eventually be in charge of adult services.

Likewise a small Episcopalian church in Florida received a donation of computers to create a ministry for homebound older adults. Soon these adults were using the internet to connect with the world. This ministry enlisted the expertise of its teens to repair the computers, distribute them, and then engage in training sessions with the seniors over a period of months.

The possibilities are endless for congregations of all sizes to present an à la carte menu—rather than a set menu that all must choose no matter what their tastes or interests are. As long as the choices are offered with guidance and accountability, such programs can deepen participation and lead to greater spiritual maturity.

Make Sure the Rewards Aren't Limited to Heaven

The Bible has fifty-nine different commands for what the followers of Jesus are to do toward "one another." The most stated command is to love one another. The second-most repeated is to encourage one another. Romans Chapters 12 to 16 give many specific examples of how believers can draw positive attention to each other as encouragement. Chapter 16 concludes with Paul giving shout-outs to many specific individuals, praising them for the things God has used them to do.

The same kind of encouragement can happen in your church, and with good results. While very few participate at church, serve others, or live out their faith ministry in order to receive acknowledgments or rewards, positive feedback does serve as a helpful motivation for most. This doesn't have to take the form of pats on the back or paper certificates of appreciation. Being asked to mentor another person or being offered further training is perhaps more rewarding than being singled out for a job well done. Announcements about successful efforts can name the team members involved: think how rewarding it is to see one's name, in a local newspaper, as part of a successful community service team. Public acknowledgment of involvement or successful ministries not only builds the confidence of those involved but also advertises the range of ministries available to others, and puts faces to service opportunities in case others are interested in joining. Any way the church leadership can spread the good news of being involved, and recognize participation, can potentially increase further commitment.

Economists and sociologists compare commitment, such as church involvement, to a balance of exchanges. The logic says that when I'm adequately rewarded for my expenditures, I'm more satisfied with the transaction. The more satisfied, the more likely I am to increase my involvement and to tell others of this "good investment." Not everyone will respond to public praise, but virtually everyone needs to feel recognized for their efforts, their growth, and their skills. Sensitive leadership will discern appropriate ways to reward and motivate participation. Remember that the goal is spirited participation, service, and involvement that feed members' faith in ways that are intrinsically and externally rewarding.

The process of understanding and strengthening what a congregation does well in order to promote participation is not an overnight venture. There is no quick fix or immediate solution. A dynamic of diminishing participation within a congregation may have developed over decades. Likewise reversing it will also take time. Long-ingrained habits are slow to reverse, especially if those habits haven't been acknowledged publicly as detrimental.

> The goal is spirited participation, service, and involvement that feed members' faith in ways that are intrinsically and externally rewarding.

The lack of full member involvement and participation, while perceived by everyone, is seldom a recognized sin. Remember that your ideal goal is to get to the point where, like the parable of Jesus, you are reaching out, not to the other 80 percent, but to the 1 percent that is missing.

9

CREATE MORE WAYS FOR PEOPLE TO PARTICIPATE

The Twenty-third Psalm is one of the best-known chapters of the entire Bible. From beginning to end, it's very personal: "The LORD is *my* shepherd, *I* shall not be in want. He makes *me* lie down in green pastures, he leads *me* beside quiet waters, he restores *my* soul" (verses 1–3, emphasis added).

In just over one hundred words, the Lord takes his sheep through a wide range of experiences. We receive restoration, guidance, comfort, mercy, love, anointing, and greater closeness with God.

If churches, as extensions of God's care, met people at similar points of need and interest, they would generate many new paths of involvement, both for those being served and those ministering. As churches establish and develop more ways to tend their flock, they could increase the likelihood of reaching those that have wandered off.

This chapter is about opening up a wider variety of opportunities for involvement, especially ones that will address the needs of those who are not currently in full participation with the rest of the herd.

In earlier chapters we explained that member involvement is multidimensional. The ideal is for members to participate in all dimensions—attending, giving, inviting, serving, leading, developing close church friends, and more. One way to strengthen people's involvement is to add a new element for participation. This might very well require thinking outside the box, if those who are not involved avoid participation because they don't like, connect with, or feel at home in your current set of involvement options.

Therefore to reach the entire congregation you might have to contemplate doing things differently. To find ways to encourage everyone to increase their participation, you may have to expand the idea of church, find new avenues for involvement, and create different spaces in which to connect.

We urge you not to limit your church to one single model or a single "correct" way. These actions counter all the research that we have seen. Rather we argue that given the diversity of people and recognizing their many different interests, gifts, and reasons for wanting to participate, the church must use multiple strategies to reach different audiences. In this day and age a leader must assume that no two people are alike, that each of us has distinctive spiritual needs. As a parish inventory respondent affirmed, "At this point in my life I am not sure how much I want to be involved but I would not like to be pushed into greater involvement. I want to do it on my own."

Religious leaders must understand this diversity of desires and shape their church's efforts to suit those needs, to cater to "the consumer" in each member. However, a spiritual leader must not stop there but rather also educate and nurture the congregation from a superficial, self-centered, individualistic consumer mentality into a deeper understanding of the spiritual life.

This chapter offers multiple suggestions. Any of them, if implemented, should help a church increase the percentage of people who volunteer and participate. It will allow and encourage the reader or leadership team, after having assessed its own people and structures, to prayerfully select certain principles to implement in order to begin the process. This approach enables them to proceed with a sense of their own resources and an understanding of what God is calling them to do and be.

Expand What It Means to Participate

Throughout the book we use a scaled variable for involvement that combines worship attendance, giving, inviting, group participation, and number of close friends. These dimensions of collective religious life become our starting point. We suggest the following ideas, even if some sound radical, on the basis of our listening and learning about what might encourage greater participation.

Attend in Lots of Ways

When someone talks about attendance, the first thing that usually comes to mind is the Sunday (or weekend) worship service. Not surprisingly the more times that a church offers worship services, the greater the total attendance.

If increasing the number of worship services is an unrealistic expectation for the vast majority of churches, other options exist as well. Church leadership that wants to expand participation and involvement without the challenge of adding new services may want to promote all of the church's spiritual activities as worship events. In other words try reinforcing the idea that where two or more are gathered there is opportunity to participate in worship. By this we don't mean to diminish the importance of Sunday congregational worship but rather to expand the idea that other gatherings of the congregation can be moments of singing, prayer, praise, education, and other worship of God. Such gatherings need not be overly formal nor limited to the traditional hours between nine and noon on Sunday morning. In short simply include more spiritual connections in all you do: Wednesday prayer groups, Thursday Vespers services, or even a Saturday morning conservationist or community service activity.

Remember, the goal is to increase involvement, of which worship participation is a component. The more opportunities to engage in worship, the greater likelihood of connecting with a larger number of persons.

Worshiping with other Christians is of utmost importance. Worship is highly correlated with increases in all other dimensions of involvement. However, there is nothing magical about the timing of gathered worship on Sunday morning. Worship as a congregation is *what* happens collectively rather than *when* it happens. As one church member noted on the parish inventory survey:

> Worship is highly correlated with increases in all other dimensions of involvement.

> So many members of my congregation put on their faith with their "Sunday go to meeting" clothes, and then give it up by noontime on the same day. I wish [more of our church members] could experience active spiritual awakening and grow to live out their faith in their daily life and in the life of this church.

For numerous reasons discussed in Chapters Four and Five, Sunday morning may well be a detriment to many members who really want to attend. We don't mean to challenge the holiness of Sunday but to encourage the expansion of worship. Communal worship can and should happen multiple times throughout the week in both formal and casual settings. Emphasizing this can help to diminish the idea that "church" is what occurs once a week on Sunday morning.

Nothing prevents worship from being incorporated into any kind of church gathering: loosely planned outings, church-sponsored play days for parents and children, book clubs, hobby groups, or formal committee meetings. Thus a stewardship committee could begin each session, not just with prayer but also with a Bible reading, sharing of concerns, and perhaps a short teaching time.

Likewise this expanded idea of worshipful gatherings can be virtual. Some of the most innovative, technologically adept churches hold robust internet campus services. In an age where some people meaningfully connect for hours on end via Facebook, blogs, and Twitter, why not do worship with similar virtual communities? Such churches tap into generational differences and new social media norms to assist members with an expanded understanding of the congregation, their spiritual community, and the idea that worship happens whenever several members gather.

Thus Facebook group gatherings, blog discussions, podcasts, and even e-mail discussions can be cast as worshipful moments—both social and solitary virtual events can become moments for praise, prayer, and collective worship of God. Teach people that worship in your congregation can occur on Sunday morning and much more often, as collective events in the community become expressive moments of grace and faith.

Giving Need Not Be Limited to Dollars

Rituals have power, not just in what they imply but in how they shape our thinking. Seeing the offering plate passed aisle by aisle reinforces that stewardship is about money. We are called to give our offering, whether pledged and delivered in an offering envelope or dropped in a bag or bucket; whether through tithing or the widow's mite. Numerous authors have tried over recent decades to expand the idea of stewardship beyond just money. We agree and suggest an expansion of the idea of giving that includes not only money but also one's talents and that most precious contemporary commodity: our time. Again the idea is to increase involvement, not to balance a budget. A church doesn't want its laid-off members avoiding congregational gatherings—and missing a critical supportive community— because they don't have money to contribute, especially in difficult economic times.

The membership has so much more to contribute to God, to the church, than just a few coins. An expansive understanding of stewardship might include embracing a "barter mentality" within the church. Emphasize the equality of giving one's trade skills, expertise, and abilities to giving money. A budget can be balanced by cheerfully given labor as well as it can through cash. Likewise volunteering one's interests and skills is probably more fulfilling and spiritually invigorating than discharging an economic obligation when times are tight. Additionally the seemingly ubiquitous demand to give money is often a huge mental hang-up for someone who has avoided church for a while. Some churches suggest to new people that they not give when they first come, but does the same apply to those who are wanting to be wooed back into the faith community?

For many people time is even more precious than money, as these women in the parish inventory survey complained:

> I hope that more [of our congregation] can find time in their busy lives to be more involved in their spiritual journey as a church family.

> I have not attended church in some time. Mostly this is connected with a selfish preservation of free time. I work some on the weekends . . . so I am overly guarded about my energy.

Recognize and acknowledge that time is precious. This is true even for those who are more able to give generously of their time, such as retirees or stay-at-home parent volunteers. Leaders should not take these folks for granted. The more people's gifts of time are highlighted, the more abundant the offerings. We often highly esteem major donors of funds; why not those who freely offer their time as well?

If giving time is a significant problem, consider how to leverage technological innovations that will increase people's ability to participate. The use of a church's website, Google Docs, or e-mail can save a lot of time by greatly reducing the need to drive to church for documents, brochures, schedules, or material to proof and edit. Technologies like Skype and Go to Meeting can substitute for face-to-face gatherings or diminish committee busywork, so that the physical gathering can be more productive and spiritually richer.

In suburbia much of our precious time is spent driving. If you reduce your members' driving time as much as possible, they will have more time for family and church.

Likewise consider tapping into ways for members with transportation difficulties to serve remotely or virtually. Stay-at-home parents or homebound members may joyfully respond to requests to stuff envelopes, connect with others through the phone, implement a card ministry, or do cooking for upcoming events. Such creative adaptations in the act of stewardship create feelings of worth, contribution, and involvement while also allowing one to participate in ways that are flexible and customizable to one's gifts, interests, and schedule. A broadening of the idea of giving may indeed create many more cheerful givers.

Any Small Grouping Can Be a "Small Group"

Humans need social involvement, and yet today there are strong cultural forces against it and fewer opportunities for it to happen. Interaction with others in the congregation solidifies commitment. Thus participation will be enhanced as more members participate in groups; this includes groups of all sizes but especially small, intimate gatherings. We've already suggested that all group involvement could be recharacterized to include acts of worship.

Unfortunately many congregations structure small-group gatherings so that they appeal predominantly to the more-active members. Could church leadership consider other ways to diversify and expand a ministry of small-group offerings, including options that address the needs of less-involved church members? In your church these needs would have been identified through your Listening Team's findings (Chapter Four). Examples might include playgroups for stay-at-home parents, educational or professional development seminars, retiree breakfast clubs, or hobby and special interest groups. All can become both fellowship and worship moments.

With publicity from a "small-group fair" plus personal invitation, these informal, small-scale gatherings can be attractive, low-commitment, and unobtrusive ways for long-lost members to reenter the congregation as more-active participants. Such groups also function well as alternative doors into the church for new persons. Not only do such groups draw on common interests and perhaps longtime connections between active and inactive members, but they are less embarrassing and anxious avenues into the church community following a long absence. Such hobby, talent, and professional development groups can also highlight the special skills and leadership abilities of less-involved members, coaxing them to increase their involvement. Consider beginning small with a onetime, short-term, or perhaps "special lecture" series on hobbies. These will help you identify potential interest groups. Invite someone to share his stamp-collecting passion, someone else to demonstrate her favorite apps on the IPod, another to lead a bird-watching hike, or someone to show how to use do-it-yourself tax software in the weeks before April 15.

> Informal small-scale gatherings can be attractive, low-commitment, and unobtrusive ways for long-lost members to reenter the congregation as more-active participants.

Another way to expand small-group possibilities at the church is to take advantage of existing community groups where members naturally gather. If countless families are torn between involvement and participation in youth sports practices and games, take the church to *them* and make it a both-and experience. At any youth league sports event, large clusters of parents gather and talk.

Don't let their potentially difficult decision to choose between sports and church sideline their participation. It should not be difficult to encourage a few key parents, with some guidance from leadership, to draw other church parents into faith-informed conversations about good sportsmanship, healthy eating, time-management, parenting skills, and mutual spiritual support. This need not be obvious or attention-getting to be an effective way of bringing the congregation together, including less-involved people.

Being a congregation "without walls" will contribute to strengthening participation levels beyond the "box" of Sunday morning. Blurring the distinction between Sunday morning "church" and a 24/7 spiritual congregation is not only biblically sound; it is also effective in creating greater participation.

Serve Where You Are

Every comparative study conducted of active Christians identifies that they are more altruistic, generous, and helpful than the unchurched nonbeliever. Members of church communities daily perform random acts of kindness, whether that is motivated intrinsically by learned virtue or speaks to a Christian commitment being lived out actively. Yet very seldom are such individual actions highlighted or seen as an extension of the expression of faith observed in a congregation. Does your church make a distinction between the service and ministry outreach of one member, several volunteers, or the entire congregation? In each case it is a part of the congregation living out its commitment to others through faithful actions. As such the church could choose to collectively celebrate these actions. This expands what ministry to others means, and again takes the faith—the "churchiness" of members—outside the box of traditional church ministry.

One such church, The Rock, which is a megachurch in San Diego, did just that and found that when it added up the individual ministry acts of its attenders, virtually the entire congregation had been engaged in service. The next year Pastor Miles McPherson challenged attenders to increase their efforts, thereby promoting wider involvement while simultaneously raising the bar on living out their faith.

While this may seem an artificial way of increasing involvement, that is because we often think of faithful outreach as only what the church sanctions. Hasn't the phenomenon of hands-on mission trips generated a renewed vigor about service to others? How might motivation further shift if more members thought of their quiet lives of spiritually motivated service to others as part of an expansive ministry of the congregation? Even those members serving in secular volunteer positions, such as sports coaches, teachers, board members, and blood donors can come to see what they do as an integral, if not explicitly overt, expression of their spiritual life. After all isn't giving a paper cup of water in God's name to a marathon runner an expression of spiritual care of our fellow humans?

Do Better Networking

Enhancing participation isn't just about expanding or nuancing programs. It's also about strengthening the ties that bind the congregation together as a caring community. Every church needs to find new ways to create and maintain these connections. This includes tried-and-true methods but also new approaches to social networking applied to the congregational community. It also means being accountable to these connections, attentive to the webs of relationships that unite, and responsive when intervention is necessary.

Enthusiasm Is Contagious

It almost goes without saying that if your church implements any of these expanded ways of being involved, your members will begin to ask long-lapsed and new persons to the church. If folks are excited about what they are doing at church, they will tell their friends. No matter what your faith tradition, evangelism of some sort is essential. Remember, people connect to the church—whether they are returning through the backdoor or through the front door for the first time—because of personal invitation. Therefore whether it is an intentional outreach to wayward sheep or members excitedly reconnecting with friends, the message that the church is expanding its participation should reach the less involved. Invite currently active members to reconnect with old friends they haven't seen in a while, not just to come to church but also to share their activities of faithful living. Folks can be invited to join their friends in service, book clubs, or any of the newly augmented small groups the church is starting, even going to see a child's or grandchild's sports event. The more doors that open into the full life of the congregation, the greater the likelihood that you will see people back and participating; but only if an effort is made to ask them back, and only if they see that the "box" they left for whatever reason is now bigger.

Wait Till You Hear the Good News: I've Gained Weight!

How often has anyone said this to you? Yet that is exactly what will have to happen to increase involvement. The leadership team will need to make the church fatter with possibilities for participation. At the same time the church must spread this good news about the expanding possibilities for participation as widely as possible. This may be easier said than done for a small church or one with a thinly stretched budget and too few volunteers. Even among large or resource-abundant congregations it is often a daunting task to create new ministries or to reinvigorate long-established ones. However, expanding what a church offers for member involvement need not be complex, nor must it entail making new programs.

As we noted in the last chapter, assessing whether everyone who is currently volunteering is happy may give longtime volunteers the opportunity and excuse to move to more fulfilling ministry roles. This alone can create openings for persons who always wanted to sing or teach but were kept out by a full roster of permanent regulars. Another way to add space without eviction is to create alternates, "stand-ins," and apprentice volunteers in key roles that are otherwise always full. Instituting mentoring, if there is a need, can also easily increase the available opportunities without starting new programs.

However, often what you currently offer by way of service, leadership, ministry, or committee work may not be appealing to or fulfilling for those who are uninvolved. If they were excited about serving in those ways, they probably would already be serving. On the basis of the gifts and talents assessments from the previous chapter your team may now have a better idea of the interests of the broader congregation. What opportunities for service or even leadership have been neglected in the congregation's history?

Expanding the available positions, however, is effective only if they are announced to the entire church, including those who seldom or never come. Hold gatherings, advertise verbally and in print, send e-mails, and post to your website calls for service that provide information about committee work and duties, jobs, repairs, or tasks that need to be done around the church. As one inventory respondent suggested: "We are all very different people with different needs. Advertising the diversity of these services and offerings in a non-tired way is very important to get different people involved." And as we found in the survey data, the most effective avenues to participation are to ask involved members to encourage their less-committed friends and appeal directly to an individual's own initiative that being a mature Christian means service and participation.

Network Your Programs

Don't think only about what your congregation can offer for involvement; also consider "outsourcing" participation to venues external to the church. The ultimate goal is to expand opportunities for service and participation in ways that connect with members' passions and talents to live out their faith. Consider acting on these potential outside interests by creating partnerships with existing local clubs, ministries, and service groups. Part of the reason for our earlier emphasis on learning about opportunities in the larger local context was to have you prayerfully consider which groups need assistance and the venues available for involvement. Invite local agencies, social service ministries, community organizations, hobby groups, clubs, schools, and welfare agencies, and perhaps even neighboring church ministries, to a ministry fair. Excite your members with the local community's needs, the wide array of involvement venues, and the range of choices of times, locations, and activities available.

Learn to think about your participation options in a "flat world" way. Your congregation, no matter what the size or level of resources, can't provide a wide enough spectrum of activities to appeal to all the interests and passions of your congregational members. You have to network with other agencies and draw on the strengths and opportunities afforded by other organizations. Even if you are the size of a mom-and-pop store, think like a mall. A mall contains very few anchor stores (what must be done to keep the church afloat), a number of tenant shops (what else we can do, but not absolutely critical), and many small kiosks (what our individual members want to accomplish through their initiative). Then consider the wider economic sector. Which boutiques and distributors (special interest, social service, and volunteer groups) should we partner with (outsource to)?—because we don't, can't, and shouldn't do it all ourselves.

Expand Your Social Networks

In many ways it is all about personal relationships. While we found that having friends at the church is less predictive of a high level of involvement than one might think, nevertheless personal connections figure prominently throughout this book. People are introduced to the church through personal ties. Many are asked to be involved by someone they know (although less than staff and leadership think!). Friendships help create a sense of belonging, offer care and support, share one another's burdens, and form a community of memory that knits lives together in a strong web of relationships. Even in the midst then of the centrifugal force of the modern world and an atomizing technological culture, a church striving for increased participation should expand its relationship-building capacities. Again think in terms of networks, especially "social networks," a buzzword of the early twenty-first century.

For whatever reasons, many participants are less connected, even disconnected. A renewed effort has to be made to connect these people to other church participants *and* to the church. There are countless low-cost and motivating ways to let marginal members know that others are there for them and that the church cares. With a simple database program and a card-sending ministry, all members can know that the congregation is thinking about them on their birthdays and anniversaries, and at times of illness or at deaths in the family. The only church one of us attended that acknowledged birthdays and anniversaries (with a hand-signed card from the senior pastor) was a massive megachurch—not one of nine other small and midsized congregations he attended did this. Technology and careful ministerial planning also allow pastoral care, through well-defined care teams and prayer chains, to augment the more mechanical efforts. A church, no matter its size, should consider instituting a "buddy system" reminiscent of swimming buddies in summer camp. This isn't as formal as mentorship (which is also a great idea), but it does ensure that all

> There are countless low-cost and motivating ways to let marginal members know that others are there for them and that the church cares.

members of the church have at least one person watching out for them, caring about them, and being aware of them.

The goal is to increase the interconnections between members. Among the technologically adept this can happen through a multitude of social medias, including the church's website, Facebook pages, blogs, Yahoo groups, e-mail distribution lists, targeted e-mail notices, and countless other platforms yet to be invented. But similar ties and connections can be created in non-virtual ways as well. Bulletin boards in the church or articles in a newsletter can announce local happenings that include members. All these means can increase the knowledge of what's happening in the congregational body and spread news about our members. Knowledge about other members solidifies relational ties; indeed if the church isn't proactive, gossip fills these gaps. Make sure the church community celebrates the joys of births, sport and school achievements, and business successes and shares the pain of illnesses and deaths. The more a church thinks of itself as an extended family—and the more it knows and is known by others—the more likely a greater percentage of the people will participate.

Be a Bridge over Troubled Waters

If these relational ties become strengthened, they can also expand and stretch in times of change and disconnection. Our analysis of data indicated that participation often decreases during times of change, whether it was leaving a committee position, a child's birth, a move to college, divorce, or relocation. We heard many comments about the lack of connections at these times of transition.

> I originally joined with my family. However, after leaving for college and moving elsewhere I have grown apart from the church.

> I would love feeling involved in the church and would love to see a strengthened outreach program for youth group that participates

past confirmation. The end years of high school seem to dwindle enthusiasm and as a part of that group, I wish that I had the same involvement that I did while being confirmed.

Tenuous moments, whether minor or serious, are occasions when disconnection from the congregation is most likely to happen. Whether due to increased distance from church, social fragmentation, pulling away from responsibilities, or physical or mental conditions, such separations are real and affect involvement negatively. Just when help is most needed, it is often not requested. A church can and should anticipate these fractures in community involvement. When a leadership team can create bridges across life changes, it stands a greater opportunity to address even the unspoken needs of members and diminish the threat of disconnection from community or loss of faith in times of greatest need.

Think for a moment about mundane life changes that can create opportunities for disconnection from the congregation. Where are the exit ramps in your church? If your congregation has been hemorrhaging its youth, what bridges might be constructed to support teens as they move from confirmation classes to adult responsibilities; from getting their driver's license to driving themselves and other teens to church; from high school graduation to back-from-college reunions with friends? If the church is more involved in these momentous changes, including encouraging newly baptized or confirmed youth into mentored leadership roles, the likelihood of losing them diminishes.

Likewise how many churches create crossover paths for persons moving from single to married status in the congregation? No doubt there are more of these than there are supportive path from being married to getting divorced. Supporting persons who are dealing with the death of a significant other is common, but what about those who are caring for a disabled family member, or those whose spouse has moved to a nursing home or homebound state. What of the emotional void of empty nesters—shouldn't the church address their needs as well? All of these life occasions provide moments for the congregation to address needs, solidify the ties of the community, and if not increase participation at least avoid the social disconnect that can result in decreased involvement.

Finally, in the era of high technology even relocation across the country can be a moment to maintain and expand the ties of a church community. Congregations may both mourn and celebrate a family's move, but do they also help it locate a new church community, continue to support it spiritually through e-mails, cards, calls, and connections on Facebook, and through inquiries into the family's new life? Or is the family now out of sight, out of mind, out of the fellowshipping community? You can leverage technology and the interests of congregational members to create, expand, and maintain personal connections. The more threads in the social fabric, the less likely someone is to slip through the holes in the congregation's blanket of community.

> The more threads in the social fabric, the less likely someone is to slip through the holes in the congregation's blanket of community.

Add Accountability: Track Your Sheep

With a strengthened social network and a buddy system where folks watch out for and care for each other, accountability among members will increase. The greater the accountability, the less traffic the back door will get. It is far easier to reach folks when they are decreasing their involvement and becoming marginal than after they have completely left the active church community. Thus a church leadership that cares about its entire congregation will institute methods of creating accountability. Many of the earlier suggestions in this book will have begun that process—doing a church census, connecting with all members, building a database, offering a gifts test, strengthening small-group ministries, creating a buddy system, and so on—yet there is still the chance that people will gradually slide off the map. We suggest every church to consider a simple three-prong approach to member accountability: track, feed back, and react.

1. *Track.* Be intentional about keeping records. Give someone, or a team, the responsibility for maintaining a database of participation and involvement. Consider a simple sign-in sheet in each row of seats or pews. Such a device not only records who is there but can be used to help congregational members learn each other's names or to collect visitor information. Additionally offering envelopes, prayer-request forms, attendance sheets at ministries and classes, and rolls from events and activities all assist in tracking the involvement of everyone. While some of these methods suggest a "big brother" watchfulness, if we serve a God who cares for each bird and flower, shouldn't church leadership do all it can to care for every member?

2. *Feed back.* If patterns of decreased or even increasing involvement are identified in the tracking process, these should be directed back to those responsible for pastoral care. Empowered lay individuals, ministry teams, or clergy should evaluate these patterns. An attempt to understand a change in a member's life is the first step in accurately addressing the person. Ideally a team of trained members, perhaps those sensitive, spiritually mature, and prayerful, responsible persons from the Listening Team, would meet monthly to assess the participatory health of the congregation, noting members who require follow-up—or celebration. We've jokingly thought of this group as the "sheepdogs" or the "99ers," or perhaps the "1-percent solution team," or maybe even the "first-alert responder team," but whatever these folks are called, they are responsible both for making sure church leadership is aware of the health of the membership and for following up on participation change.

3. *React.* Identification and assessment are necessary, but they are useless unless actions are taken to address participation shifts. On the positive side, increased involvement should

trigger some level of acknowledgment. A church need not hand out awards or stroke the egos of those who are doing what is expected of the Christian believer, but at the same time we've noted that rewarded participation results in strengthened commitment levels. On the other side, the sooner decreases in participation are identified and addressed, the less likely a member will disconnect. Don't let known situations of discontent fester into wounds that will never heal. Don't let the sun set on your congregational members' anger. Whether declining involvement is the result of life situations, personal issues, or discontent, don't allow it to extend weeks or months without intervention, and hopefully resolution. Don't forget: marginal members are much easier to engage while still marginally involved; once gone, they are much harder to return to the fold.

Peek into a Few Pandora's Boxes

God is the same yesterday, today, and forever, but our ministry approaches don't have to be. We don't want to stir up a hornet's nest of controversy with our suggestions, but again many folks have chosen not to be a part of your church "box" precisely because that box no longer fits them.

Much research on congregational life points to new expressions of the faith—such as new ways of doing worship—as being conducive to church growth, influential in promoting involvement, and attractive to new generations who are increasingly absent from the church. At the very least a few of these expressions should be included in a leadership team's thoughts about new approaches, outside of your box, to increasing the participation of members who are not currently engaged. Would adding, or changing to, a more contemporary worship format, or a contemplative prayer time, or even a "U2charist" service appeal to those who have chosen to remain at a distance? Could the invitation of a struggling immigrant group into the church result perhaps in a blended multiracial congregation that signaled to marginal members the congregation's openness and embrace of diversity?

Would creating a satellite service or planting a daughter church near a distant group of members encourage them to become more involved? And would the additional leadership positions provide an avenue for members to fill these roles, learn new skills, and simultaneously develop greater spiritual maturity?

Finally would creating an internet ministry team attract younger members who have tech skills while also helping to bring to fruition many of our earlier technological suggestions? These and many other more innovative directions should be explored and considered. While most of the more radical suggestions will engender controversy and possibly conflicts (an opening of Pandora's box that could lead to decreased participation), if alternatives to the "traditional church box" are never considered, future generations will no longer participate at all. As one young adult's comment pointedly reminded us,

> I feel like . . . the church . . . needs a lot [of] help but seems like is afraid to take new ideas from some[one] like me who's much younger and has been there first hand. If the church doesn't seriously start taking new ideas and listen to the people who know this church, the problems will get worse.

Whatever approaches your leadership team chooses to help create greater participation, they should fit your context and resources. Guided by your seeking God's will for this congregation, the effort should be driven by your faith in living out the vision of serving God and God's people in this flock. This is serious business, as one inventory comment reminds us:

> Religion and church attendance is voluntary, as such; people attend because they want to participate. Any change has consequences, some unintended. Please be conscious of how we reach

out to people and not alienate the ones that regularly participate. . . . Let's not push anyone away.

The effort must rest in a collective commitment of the
entire church and leadership not to let anyone drift away without a response from the congregational body. This will require
intentional work, attention, and vigilance, but above all it
demands a serious spiritual commitment to care for the entire
body of Christ. So it is to this reminder that we turn in the final
chapter.

10

REACH TOWARD SPIRITUAL
GROWTH AND DEVELOPMENT

I (Warren) know a woman who found a church during her fresh-man year of college. She became quite active there, experienc-ing a great deal of spiritual growth through the congregation. After graduation she remained in the area and continued to be involved in that church.

This friend is outgoing and friendly, so she would always make it a point to welcome newcomers. The church had 100–150 people, making it quite easy for her to recognize some-one as new.

The church changed pastors during my friend's fifth year there. A few weeks later a most interesting exchange happened in the church's fellowship area. My friend greeted another woman whom she had never seen. Each introduced herself to the other. The woman's name was Mae Jo. Then my friend politely asked, "Is this your first time here?"

"Oh, no," Mae Jo replied indignantly. "I'm a charter member."

Confused, my friend replied, "But I've never seen you here before."

Mae Jo didn't offer further comment. She just kind of smiled and walked on. My friend wasn't sure what to say either, so she was glad Mae Jo moved on!

That event occurred over twenty years ago. Since then I've learned that episodes like this are not isolated. It turns out that charter member Mae Jo did not like the previous pastor. She chose to wait until the next pastor came, and made a fresh start then.

For five years she had dropped her kids off at the church's youth group, but had not herself reappeared. Even though she returned to the church with some unresolved baggage from the past, isn't this circumstance something we have all experienced at one level or another?

This situation represents the idea that although many people are connected with a church, their participation is more like that of a spectator than an active disciple. Some are total no-shows. Others participate minimally at best.

Yet sometimes a trigger event brings them back. Maybe it's an invitation from a friend in the church. Perhaps it's a life crisis. In this case it was curiosity about the new pastor, supported by the prayers and modeling from her sons in the youth group and ongoing involvement during the interim with a few long-time members at that church.

The existence of nonattending members seems bizarre or contradictory to many active churchgoers like my friend; yet there are literally millions of people who are members but do not attend. If you roughly compare the percentage of people who say they are members of a church (65%) against the percentage who say they attend regularly (40%), the difference translates into big numbers: we estimate there are about thirty-eight million inactive adult church members in the United States.

> We estimate there are about thirty-eight million inactive adult church members in the United States.

Looking for Spiritual Maturity

This book has been about the group we've called the other 80 percent. They're represented by Mae Jo and millions of others. Each has a different story. We've focused on how to understand them and how to bring them toward greater involvement in your church.

But that's not enough. Our purpose in this final chapter is to affirm that increased involvement is certainly not the ultimate goal for these wayward and sometimes lost sheep. Yes, it was a positive step when a charter member at my friend's church came back. Mae Jo began coming somewhat regularly to the weekly worship service and at times to Sunday school. She became a deaconess, part of a group that serves others in need, such as families with a new baby or households with a major illness. She reconnected with other longtime members. Maybe she even made some new friends among the congregation.

While these are positive steps, the bigger issue is whether Mae Jo (and similar representatives of the other 80 percent) grew spiritually. Did she work on forgiving the previous pastor? Through her renewed church activities did she engage with God at deeper levels? Did she become a more active disciple of Jesus Christ? Did she become spiritually revitalized to love God more with her heart, mind, and soul? Did she have more love for her neighbor? Did she grow in the grace of Christ through the transforming power of the Holy Spirit?

Involvement Equals Spiritual Growth Equals Involvement

Surveys of church people clearly indicate an important reality about people who are highly committed: the most involved are also most likely to say they are spiritually fulfilled, to acknowledge spiritual growth, and to express satisfaction with their journey of faith. There is a strong, unmistakable relationship between the two.

> The most involved are also most likely to say they are spiritually fulfilled.

The million-dollar question is, Which comes first, church involvement or spiritual growth? Theology certainly gives insight into this issue. From a researcher's point of view it's hard to know which developed first. The answer seems to vary by individual. Some folks "fake it till they make it." The change happens as they get involved and hang out with other strong believers.

Their spiritual passions and disciplines grow. They see God more at work in them and through them. Others have a profound spiritual experience that leads them to considerable service and dedication.

We saw this repeatedly in our focus groups, even in the same household. One person had a spiritual hunger that caused the whole family to go church shopping, one spouse loving the quest and the other going through the motions. Then over time it genuinely connected with him or her as well. We also saw such contrast in a Christ-centered recovery group we attended, a major outreach of a certain church. The man on one side of us started with church involvement, which led to spiritual growth, which led to his dealing with his recovery. The man on the other side of us first came because of his need for recovery, which led to spiritual growth, which led to church involvement.

Whichever the case, the most important point for church leadership is to know that the two realities are highly correlated. They reinforce each other. For the vast majority of people, the more fulfilling their worship and ministry experiences, relationships in smaller groups, and so forth are, the more likely they are to describe themselves as growing spiritually. Likewise the more they are spiritually satisfied, as through growing in faith, developing as spiritual leaders, and using the gifts and talents God has given them, the more likely they are to be attending, giving, volunteering, and inviting others to experience what they are receiving spiritually.

Where to start and which to emphasize? In essence the role of church leaders is to coach people toward spiritual maturity. As Scripture teaches, God "gave some to be apostles, some to be prophets, some to be evangelists, and some to be *pastors and teachers*, to prepare God's people for works of service, so that the body of Christ may be built up until we all reach unity in the faith and in the knowledge of the Son of God and *become mature*, attaining to the whole measure of the fullness of Christ" (Ephesians 4:11–13, emphasis added).

The Other 80 Percent has emphasized that it's not enough for church leadership to assist only the 20 percent who want to grow, as important as that is. The leaders' web of spiritual responsibility extends far beyond the portion of the flock who volunteer or even show up weekly. *All* members of the congregation—everyone who claims any affiliation with a church—deserve and need its spiritual care, no matter how irregularly they show up.

Efforts to encourage greater participation are only one aspect of improving the spiritual life of a church's flock. Even so, the data in our research seem to imply that such spiritually motivated efforts are really two sides of the same coin.

Perhaps the best image is that of a cycle. As people become involved, they will grow spiritually, as long as you're trying in every way possible to build their spiritual life, and hopefully doing so for your entire flock. Likewise as you help more people participate, the vast majority will also grow spiritually. This book has talked a lot about participation because that part of the cycle is easier to measure. Always remember though that the ultimate purpose of participation is spiritual growth, which is more important to God—even if it's harder for statisticians like us to measure!

> *All* members of the congregation—everyone who claims any affiliation with a church—deserve and need its spiritual care, no matter how irregularly they show up.

Pushing Against Pareto

We introduced the 80/20 Pareto Principle in the Introduction of this book. The ratio seems true for many areas of life. Our point at the beginning of the book was that churches do not need to be limited to any 80/20 rule.

Now we need to warn that even if you succeed in reversing Pareto by involving 80 percent of the congregation, or perhaps

90, or even 100, your high participation level will not naturally remain that way. If you're not diligent and do not guide all people to engage (and not just those who want to be involved), then participation will decrease, and the 80/20 situation will happen again. If things are left to their own devices, then Pareto will rule.

If things are left to their own devices, then Pareto will rule.

Pareto can also win in another way. If you place participation at the forefront of the church's life but do so for self-serving or need-based motives only, your push will likewise work only for a season. People's energy will wane unless you connect their involvement to a spiritual end. The way to keep Pareto at bay is for a church's leadership to be truly committed to being a spiritual shepherd, always connecting activity with some aspect of spiritual maturity.

Spiritual growth and fulfillment are indeed a spiritual quest. Taking care of your sheep means developing their spiritual lives. Jesus taught that "small is the gate and narrow the road that leads to life" (Matthew 7:13–14), but each individual has to find a different way along that narrow path.

When that happens, you will hear with increasing frequency positive testimonies like this one recorded in a Hartford Institute parish profile:

> I recently returned to church this past spring. I had been unhappy for many years. I am excited to see and feel the enthusiasm of the congregation as we reach forward. The energy, the comfort, the reverence, the creativity, the tradition, the warmth, the CONNECTION has returned, and most importantly the WORD is being taught and people are taking action within the church. The youth are growing, the young families are visiting, and members are returning. I do want to continue in this manner. The pastoral staff has come alive and been allowed to grow and create and respond to the people. . . . The sermons not

only teach from the Bible but [they also] touch us in our daily lives with examples.

This individual used all capital letters to emphasize the words CONNECTION and WORD. Is this the kind of person you would want in your congregation? If so, then continue to care for the 20 percent who are already involved. Continue your efforts to reach people with no connection to God or a church. But also, do make time, do commit the energy and do set the priority to be spiritually responsible for those we call the other 80 percent. Only then will your church's shepherding come close to the standard that Jesus modeled in his parable of the lost sheep: the flock stays together in healthy ways, and when even one sheep wanders off, every effort is made to bring it back.

Afterword

The Sheep Who Came Back into the Fold

It came to pass that a shepherd became increasingly troubled by the condition of his flock. He had been most faithful at walking to the barn each morning, opening the doors, and warmly greeting all the sheep. Then he would urge each one to follow him out to green pastures and still waters. Each evening he would lead the herd back to the barn, though usually it wasn't exactly the same group that had started the morning with him. For during the day a few sheep had wandered off. Some previous wanderers had returned. And some made it clear that they didn't particularly want to follow their shepherd's guidance, preferring instead to hang out with the stray sheep in the area.

"Something's not working right," the shepherd kept sensing. His flock numbered one hundred, at least in theory. About twenty served as the core of the flock—they comfortably hung out with each other; they wanted to grow and be healthy; and they produced a harvest of fluffy wool.

The other 80 percent were quite a mix. Many weren't very engaged with the life of the flock; some showed up only two or three times a year, if that. Most grew shabby coats of wool. A few even ran away whenever it was time for shearing.

The shepherd took stock of his situation and decided to make some changes. His first decision was to view all one hundred sheep as his charge. They might vary in their needs and their responses to him and the other sheep, but he'd take responsibility for the well-being of all of them.

So each day while his core of twenty were safely grazing, he left them so that he could spend time with the other sheep, the wanderers, and the wild, "unflocked" sheep. Each evening as the flock trekked back to the barn, he made a point to greet them warmly as they passed by. He called each sheep by name, wanderers and stray sheep alike. Many times he would invite them to join the flock and come to their home.

Over time not all one hundred sheep came back into the active fold, but many did, including a few strays who had never been part of any flock. The overall flock developed a healthier look, and indeed they were healthy.

But the shepherd never grew satisfied enough to return to his previous habit of caring for the active sheep only. He continued to make it a priority each day to leave the flock and go looking, knowing that his search was worthwhile even if for just one lost sheep.

In fact he trained many undershepherds to care for a portion of the flock. And for the rest of his years, just as the parable of Jesus modeled, he and all those he trained would "leave the ninety-nine on the hills and go to look for the one that wandered off" (Matthew 18:12).

Appendix A

RESOURCES

Surveys Suitable for Listening Teams
(Chapter Three and Appendix C)

Hartford Institute Parish Inventories
http://www.hartfordinstitute.org/leadership/church_inventory
.html

For thirty years the Hartford Institute for Religion Research has offered three types of inventories for churches to survey their membership. The Parish Profile, Church Planning, and Pastoral Search Inventories can be done in print or online. These inventories include sections dealing with tasks of the church, organizational processes, congregational identity, church facilities, and members' backgrounds, as well as theological and faith practice characteristics. The online version is customizable. The Hartford Institute is now also offering a version of its Inventory that measures a congregation's involvement and participation levels based on the questions used extensively in this book.

The U.S. Congregational Life Survey
http://www.uscongregations.org/survey.htm

Since 2001 the organization U.S. Congregations has been surveying churches and making their survey instrument available for use by any congregation. This survey instrument is in print and is designed to be distributed and completed during worship services. The results provided to each congregation include several customized comparative reports and books. Used extensively in this book.

Online Mapping of Member Addresses (Chapter Three)

batchgeo

http://www.batchgeo.com/

This website allows the user to download an Excel spreadsheet, which can be used to import a set of address data (names, group labels, e-mail addresses, and other data) before pasting it back into the site section labeled "Step 1: Source Data." User presses the validate button to make sure the columns are recognized properly, then verifies that the geocoding application has properly recognized user's columns for geocoding under Step 2. Finally, user clicks the "Run Geocoder" button; after the records are processed, a geocoded map of user's addresses will appear on the page.

gpsvisualizer

http://www.gpsvisualizer.com/geocoder/

This website is slightly more complex than batchgeo.com but also allows considerably more flexibility. It lets user input user's comma-delimited address list by uploading it or by cutting and pasting the information. Once the data are entered, user presses the button to geocode the addresses. User is then able to draw a map of these addresses, including varying the display by selecting styles, point sizes, colors, and map format.

Software

OrgAction (http://www.orgaction.com/org/)

Online scheduling, tracking, and customized solutions for volunteer management.

Volunteer2 (http://www.Volunteer2.com/)

Fostering growth in the volunteer sector. Offers tools for recruiting, tracking, scheduling, and so on.

Volunteer Software (http://www.volsoft.com/)

Software for organizing your volunteers.

VolunteerHub (http://www.volunteerhub.com/)

Web-based service for event and volunteer management, such as an online registration process.

Your Volunteers (http://www.yourvolunteers.com/), Primary Key Technologies, Inc.

A web-based volunteer management application designed particularly for special events.

Church Windows (http://www.churchwindows.com/shop/), Computer Helper Publishing of Columbus

Member management software.

MVP (http://www.filebuzz.com/fileinfo/59083/MVP.html), Sapientech

Allows the user to enter and store volunteer/member information, event information, and contribution information into a database. As events are entered, volunteers/members can be assigned to these events, reports can be generated, and so on.

Attendance Management System (http://www.filebuzz.com/fileinfo/58472/Attendance_Management_System.html), Joel Roggenkamp

Keeps track of attendance for community organizations.

Online Resources

Best Church Practices: Volunteer Applications (http://www.BuildingChurchLeaders.com), Christianity Today International, 2005

Training Pack—With better volunteer applications, your church will be more likely to find the right people and to help those people find the right position, all while carefully limiting your risk. These forms can be altered, customized, and printed out to make your application process more thorough, safe, and legal.

Best Church Practices: Church Volunteer Evaluations (http://www.BuildingChurchLeaders.com), Christianity Today International, 2005

Training Pack—These forms will help your volunteers review their goals and objectives as well as evaluate whether they are using their spiritual gifts. You can alter, customize, and print out each form to make your evaluations a smooth and helpful process.

Children's Ministry: Recruit and Train Volunteers (http://www.BuildingChurchLeaders.com), Christianity Today International, 2005

Recruiting and retaining children's workers doesn't have to be impossible.

Children's Ministry: What Every Volunteer Needs (http://www.BuildingChurchLeaders.com), Christianity Today International, 2005

Whether you're recruiting, retaining, or discipling volunteers, this tool unveils how to get them to serve faithfully and joyfully for years.

Church Volunteer Central (http://www.churchvolunteercentral.com)

This website serves as an equipping center for materials related to volunteering in the church.

Directors of Church Volunteer Ministries (http://DCVM.org), 1992

A national networking website that connects church leaders interested in training and motivating volunteers.

Energy & Enthusiasm (http://www.BuildingChurchLeaders.com), Christianity Today International, 2007

Training Theme and PowerPoint—Learn how to maintain vibrancy while balancing a full life and important kingdom work.

Fellowship One (http://www.fellowshiptech.com/), Irving, TX: Fellowship Technologies, 2004

Web-based church management software.

Practical Ministry Skills: Cultivating Active Church Members (http://www.BuildingChurchLeaders.com), Christianity Today International, 2005

Leadership Resources—Brief, practical handouts are designed to give your congregation tools to help new members discover their spiritual gifts and employ them for God's kingdom.

Survival Guides: Secrets of Recruiting & Keeping Volunteers (http://www.BuildingChurchLeaders.com), Christianity Today International, 2005

Training Pack—Discover useful approaches to one of a church leader's hardest tasks: finding and keeping volunteers.

The City (http://www.onthecity.org/), Grand Rapids, MI: Zondervan, 2010

A web-based communication and administration platform for your church that empowers community and enables mission, seven days a week.

Volunteer Development (http://www.BuildingChurchLeaders .com), Christianity Today International, 2007

Training Theme and PowerPoint—Give unpaid workers in the church, who are often the lifeblood of ministry, the proper training and direction they need.

Appendix B

METHODS AND DESCRIPTION OF THE DATASETS

Throughout this book we use research from a number of different study projects. Rather than footnoting every citation, we note in the text which study the information came from.

This appendix describes the scope, sample size, and methods of each study from which we drew our information. We also point to internet locations where it is possible to find further information and conclusions drawn from these studies. If a book is directly relevant to the study, we mention that as well. We trust that by drawing on these different sources of information, we are able to provide a rich, highly credible picture of church life in the United States.

U.S. Congregational Life Survey

This survey is also referred to in this book as the "congregational life survey."

As part of the largest survey of worshipers in America ever conducted, over one hundred thousand Protestants in over two thousand congregations across the United States participated in the U.S. Congregational Life Survey. The project was conducted in two waves: in 2001, and then in 2008–2009. Three types of surveys were completed in each participating congregation: (1) an attender survey, completed by all worshipers age fifteen and older; (2) a congregational profile describing the congregation's facilities, staff, programs, and worship services, completed by one person in the congregation; and (3) a leader survey, completed by the pastor or other leader. Together the information collected provides a unique three-dimensional look at religious life in America.

The principal investigators for this study were Cynthia Woolever and Deborah Bruce, Research Services, Presbyterian Church (U.S.A.); with Ida Smith-Williams and Joelle Anderson, also of the PC (U.S.A.) Research Services office.

Related publications and resources are listed here:

Woolever, C., and Bruce, D. *Beyond the Ordinary: 10 Strengths of U.S. Congregations.* Louisville, KY: Westminster John Knox Press, 2004.
Woolever, C., and Bruce, D. *Places of Promise: Finding Strength in Your Congregation's Location.* Louisville, KY: Westminster John Knox Press, 2008.
Woolever, C., and Bruce, D. *A Field Guide to U.S. Congregations, Second Edition.* Louisville, KY: Westminster John Knox Press, 2010.

Other reports are listed at www.USCongregations.org. The data from this study are available at www.thearda.com/Archive/USCLS.asp.

Hartford Institute for Religion Research: Parish Profile Inventories

These inventories are also referred to in this book as the "parish profiles" or "parish inventories." For thirty years the Hartford Institute for Religion Research has offered three types of inventories for churches to survey their membership. These inventories include sections dealing with tasks of the church, organizational processes, congregational identity, church facilities, and members' backgrounds, as well as theological and faith practice characteristics. The Hartford Institute now offers a version of its Inventory that measures a congregation's involvement and participation levels based on the questions used extensively in this book.

The findings used in this book are from churches that used Parish Inventory forms between March 2004 and June 2010, totaling 25,091 respondents from 193 churches. A third of these churches are United Church of Christ; 29 percent are Presbyterian PC(USA); and 12 percent are Episcopal. Mainline churches make up an additional 9 percent, including Lutheran (ELCA), American Baptist, and United Methodist. The remaining roughly 14 percent are from conservative and Evangelical churches, including Southern Baptist, nondenominational, and Church of God. Their average size is in the range of 150–200 active attenders. These churches are from thirty-four states with no one state accounting for more than 10 percent of the sample. The average response rate was roughly 30 to 35 percent.

A related website is www.hartfordinstitute.org.

Megachurch Study

This study is also referred to in this book as the study of "larger churches."

This 2008–2009 research study was jointly conducted by Warren Bird of Leadership Network, Dallas, Texas (www.leadnet .org), and Scott Thumma of Hartford Seminary's Hartford Institute for Religion Research (www.hartfordinstitute.org).

During the first half of 2008, twelve megachurches were selected in an effort to typify the overall profile of America's roughly 1,400 megachurches (congregations with weekly worship attendance of two thousand or more adults and children). These twelve churches represent, as closely as possible for a group of that size, the national megachurch profile in terms of attendance, region, denomination, dominant race or multiracial character, founding date, whether they crossed the two-thousand mark under the leadership of their present senior pastor, and whether they are multisite.

In 2009 a second wave of thirteen additional churches was selected. All twenty-five churches participated in the worship attender survey of everyone age eighteen and over present in the congregational worship services at all locations on a weekend selected by the church's leadership. A number of the questions in the this congregational survey were worded to intentionally parallel questions in the Faith Communities Today 2008 Study, the U.S. Congregational Life Study, and the Parish Inventory Study.

The first twelve churches participated in the following additional research:

1. On-site visits for firsthand observation, interviews, and focus groups. We conducted 476 total interviews (352 in focus groups, and 124 individual interviews) with recent attenders, longtime attenders, key lay leaders, and senior staff, plus individually with key staff and pastors.

2. Staff survey. This involved 718 completed surveys yielding a 75 percent response rate.

3. Ex-attender surveys. Of thirty-five or so (approximately four hundred total) distributed at each church with requests that they be sent to ex-attenders, fewer than one hundred were returned.

4. Participation in the key informant Survey of North America's Largest Churches. This national survey drew approximately four hundred responses. A first public report was released in September 2008 entitled "Changes in American Megachurches." It is available for free downloading at www.hartfordinstitute.org and www.leadnet.org/megachurch.

Faith Communities Today 2008

This study is also referred to in this book as "FACT" or the "FACT study."

The research project known as Faith Communities Today 2000 (FACT) was the largest survey of congregations ever conducted in the United States. The FACT data brought together twenty-six national surveys of congregations representing forty-one denominations and faith groups, which included about 90 percent of worshipers in the United States. Participating faith groups developed a common core questionnaire. They then conducted their own surveys. More than 14,300 congregations participated in the survey. Usually a congregation's leader completed the questionnaire.

The multifaith coalition of denominations and faith groups that conducted the Faith Communities Today 2000 national study of congregations subsequently decided to continue a regular survey initiative under the name of the Cooperative Congregational Studies Partnership (CCSP), releasing research conducted in 2005 and 2008.

The FACT2008 survey samples are an aggregation of three different layers designed to represent the universe of American congregations. One layer is a mail and web survey of a random sample of three thousand U.S. congregations conducted for CCSP by the research services office of the Presbyterian Church (U.S.A.). A second layer is a telephone survey of a random sample of one thousand congregations conducted by the Center for Creative Ministry. The third layer is a set of mini surveys conducted by twelve of the CCSP partner denominations and faith groups. These mini surveys used the FACT2008 questionnaire but were conducted by the respective denomination or faith group as a supplement to the general samples. The general survey sample was generated by the CCSP Research Taskforce from a larger random national sample of congregations purchased from MCH at www.mailings.com.

The final aggregated dataset for the 2008 survey used predominantly in this book contains questionnaires from 2,527 congregations. To better represent national population parameters, a two-stage weighting procedure was used. To mitigate the overrepresentation of those denominations and faith groups that contributed supplemental survey data, the total aggregated responses were weighted to the population parameters for faith families presented by Hadaway and Marler.*

To further enhance national representation, the total aggregated dataset of FACT2008 was also weighted to size of congregation and rural/city/suburban location parameters found in the FACT2000 national survey of 14,301 congregations. This is the same weighting procedure used for FACT2005 and therefore has the added benefit of making the report's trend comparisons more robust. The sampling error for FACT2008 type samples is difficult to calculate with precision, but is estimated to be +/− 4 percent. Research findings and many topical reports from this larger project are available at http://faithcommunitiestoday.org/research-projects-findings.

Much of Chapter Five's analysis is based on the Faith Communities Today 2008 study (FACT) and is informed by documents written by David Roozen and Michael McMullen, as found in this book's Annotated Bibliography. In using this dataset, we were limited by whatever questions the FACT study asked. While the survey is very rich in questions about volunteer dynamics, we were unable to create a measure of congregational participation, as we had with the individual-level data. Therefore we occasionally used the Faith Communities Today 2000 survey for this analysis, although we relied mostly on one question in the FACT2008 survey ("How easy or difficult is it for your congregation to recruit people for volunteer leadership roles; for example, serving on governing boards or committees, or teaching Sunday school?") as a substitute measure. A similar question about volunteer development in the Faith Communities Today 2000 survey, while not ideal for our task, was highly correlated with the ratio of attenders to members in a church,

---

*Hadaway, C. K., and Marler, P. L. "How Many Americans Attend Worship Each Week? An Alternative Approach to Measure." *Journal for the Scientific Study of Religion*, 2005, *44*(3), 307–22, Table 2.

from that same research. Additionally, we reduced the Protestant sample to include only mainline, Evangelical, and African American churches; therefore our figures for Protestants are somewhat different from the FACT2008 report itself, unless we happen to be quoting that report.

Reveal

This study is also referred to in this book as "Willow Creek's study."

Willow Creek Community Church, Barrington, IL, one of the largest and most influential churches in the United States, has created a database of surveys of churchgoers. It describes the project, named Reveal, as a discipleship framework. The purpose of the research is to provide a diagnostic tool for local church leaders to use in helping people move along a continuum of spiritual growth. Its growing database currently profiles some 280,000 congregants in more than 1,200 churches. The principals are Eric Arnson, who comes from a career in brand strategy, and Terry Schweizer, with a background in custom-market research. The formal research began in 2006, with the first findings publicly released in 2008. The website is www.revealnow .com, and the relevant publications are listed here:

Hawkins, G., and Parkinson, C. *Reveal: Where Are You?* Barrington, IL: Willow Creek Association, 2007.

Hawkins, G., and Parkinson, C. *Follow Me: What's Next For You?* Barrington, IL: Willow Creek Resources, 2008.

Hawkins, G., and Parkinson, C. *Focus: The Top Ten Things People Want and Need from You and Your Church.* Barrington, IL: Willow Creek Resources, 2009.

Appendix C

SAMPLE SURVEY QUESTIONS

If you conduct your own congregational survey to measure involvement, here are sample questions you might consider asking, along with instructions for respondents. Some of these questions we asked in the surveys we conducted for this book (described in Appendix B). Choose and adapt those most appropriate to your context.

● ● ●

Instructions: This survey is for everyone age eighteen and older present in today's service, *including first-time guests and other recent newcomers.* Please take a few minutes to help us learn about the degree to which this church is meeting your spiritual needs. As you answer, keep in mind that the survey is *anonymous.*

1. How *long* have you been going to church (worship) services or activities at this church?

Less than one year

1–2 years

3–5 years

6–10 years

More than 10 years

I am visiting from another church

I am visiting and do not regularly go anywhere

2. How *often* do you go to church (worship) services at this congregation?

This is my first time

Hardly ever or on special occasions

Less than once a month

Once a month

Two or three times a month

Usually every week (or more)

3. How has your participation in this church's activities *changed* in the last two years?

Increased

Remained the same

Decreased

I haven't been here two years

4. If your participation here has increased, which of the following are reasons for that (check all that apply):

More time available

Better health

Because of children

Stronger faith

Accepted office or other new responsibility in the church

More positive attitude toward the church

5. How often do you typically *volunteer* in any capacity at this church?

Never

Occasionally (a few times a year)

Regularly (once or twice a month)

Often (three times a month or more)

6. How many of your closest friends attend this church?

None

One

Two

Three

Four or more

7. Over the last year, how much have you grown in your faith?

No real growth

Some growth

Much growth, mainly through this congregation

Much growth, mainly through other groups or congregations

Much growth, mainly through my own private activities

8. In the past week, how often did you practice personal devotions (times of Bible reading and prayer)?

Seldom: 1 time or not at all

Often: 2–5 times

Nearly daily: 6–7 times

9. Are you regularly involved in the following group activities at this church? (Check *all* that apply)

Sunday school or church school

Prayer, spiritual discussion, or Bible study groups

Fellowships, clubs, or other social groups

Support or recovery groups

Community service or social justice groups

Other small group activities

10. During the past year, roughly how many people did you *invite* to your church? (Include people you invited even if they did not accept the invitation.)

0

1–2

3–5

6–10

More than 10

11. Marital status:

Single, never married

Married—first marriage

Remarried

Separated or divorced

Widowed

Other

12. Which statement best describes the people who currently live in your household?

I live alone

A couple without children

One adult with child/children

Two or more adults with child/children

Some adults living in the same household

13. About how much do you give financially to this church?

I do not contribute financially here

I give a small amount whenever I am here

I give less than 5 percent of net income regularly

I give about 5 to 9 percent of net income regularly

I give about 10 percent or more of net income regularly

14. Before you started coming to this church, were you participating at another church?

No, I've come here for most of my life

No, before coming here I had not been attending any church regularly for several years

No, before coming here I had never regularly attended

Yes, immediately prior to coming here I was participating in another church in this area

Yes, prior to coming here I was participating in a distant church, but I just moved into this area

15. To what extent do you agree or disagree with each statement as it describes your congregation?

A. My spiritual needs are being *met* in this church.

1 (strongly disagree) to 5 (strongly agree)

B. Church leaders encourage me to *discover and use* my gifts and skills for ministry and service.

1 (strongly disagree) to 5 (strongly agree)

C. This church makes a strong effort to help me get *involved* in the activities and life of the church body.

1 (strongly disagree) to 5 (strongly agree)

D. This church has made a strong effort to *train, develop or coach* me in how to be a better leader in the church.

1 (strongly disagree) to 5 (strongly agree)

E. This church has encouraged me to *serve* the wider community, nation, and world.

1 (strongly disagree) to 5 (strongly agree)

F. I have a strong sense of *belonging* to this church.

1 (strongly disagree) to 5 (strongly agree)

16. Listed below are a number of tasks that a local church is likely to perform. Please respond to each item by indicating whether you feel your congregation needs to give it more emphasis (that is, needs to do more of it or do it better); whether you are very satisfied or generally satisfied with your congregation's current performance of the task; or whether you feel the task currently receives too much emphasis?

Needs More Emphasis (4)	Very Satisfied (3)	Generally Satisfied (2)	Receives Too Much Emphasis (1)

A. Offering worship that provides a meaningful experience of God and the Christian tradition

B. Providing worship that expresses the Gospel in contemporary language and forms

C. Providing Christian education for children and youth

D. Providing Christian education programs for adults

E. Helping members deepen their personal, spiritual relationship with God

F. Sharing the good news of the Gospel with the unchurched

G. Engaging in acts of charity and service to persons in need

H. Encouraging members to act on the relationship of the Christian faith to social, political, and economic issues

I. Providing a caring ministry for the sick, shut-ins, and the bereaved

J. Providing pastoral counseling to help members deal with personal problems

K. Providing fellowship opportunities for members

L. Helping members understand their use of money, time, and talents as expressions of Christian stewardship

M. Supporting the global mission of the church/denomination

N. Helping members discover their own gifts for ministry and service

O. Participating in activities and programs with other local religious groups

P. Expressing our denominational heritage/tradition

17. Please rate your agreement or disagreement with the following statements from your perspective as an individual looking at your congregation's overall identity and vision.

Strongly Agree (4)	Agree (3)	Strongly Disagree (2)	Disagree (1)

A. Our church's identity, as it is, is one with which I feel comfortable.

B. It is easy for me to tell my friends what is unique about our church.

C. I have a clear understanding of what our church stands for.

D. An effective effort was made to instruct me in our church's mission.

E. I have a strong sense of belonging to this congregation.

F. Being at this church has made a difference in my spiritual life.

Annotated Bibliography

Baard, P., and Aridas, C. *Motivating Your Church: How Any Leader Can Ignite Intrinsic Motivation and Growth*. Chestnut Ridge, NY: Crossroad, 2001.
Easy-to-adopt insights for motivating volunteers.

Becker, P., and Dhingra, P. "Religious Involvement and Volunteering." *Sociology of Religion*, 2001, 62, 315–35.
This paper examines the role of congregations in civil society by examining the relationship between religious involvement and volunteering.

Bugbee, B. *What You Do Best in the Body of Christ: Discover Your Spiritual Gifts, Personal Style, and God-Given Passion*. Grand Rapids, MI: Zondervan, 1995.
The author offers a method to help Christians maximize their effectiveness by identifying their spiritual gifts, passions, and relational style.

Gifford, M. L. *The Turnaround Church: Inspiration and Tools for Life-Sustaining Change*. Herndon, VA: Alban Institute, 2009.
The story of Wollaston Congregational Church United Church of Christ, a once thriving church that had slowly declined and then experienced a turnaround.

Hadaway, C. K. *What Can We Do About Church Dropouts?* Nashville, TN: Abingdon Press, 1990.
How to reach church dropouts through both innovative and traditional approaches to ministry.

Hybels, B. *The Volunteer Revolution: Unleashing the Power of Everybody*. Grand Rapids, MI: Zondervan, 2004.
This book addresses why volunteers are crucial to the future of church ministry and how leaders can train and equip volunteers in their churches.

Johnson, D. *Empowering Lay Volunteers*. Nashville, TN: Abingdon Press, 1991.
This book describes how to strengthen churches by successful training of volunteers to carry out key tasks. It is a follow-up to the author's earlier book *The Care and Feeding of Volunteers*, 1978.

Kanter, R. *Commitment and Community: Communes and Utopias in Sociological Perspective*. Cambridge, MA: Harvard University Press, 1972.

An analysis of the nature and process of enduring commitment, based on the author's theory of commitment mechanisms on exhaustive research of nineteenth-century utopias, sharpened by firsthand knowledge of a variety of contemporary groups.

McMullen, M., and Roozen, D. *Insights into Integrating Congregational Members*. Forthcoming, www.faithcommunitiestoday.org.

This Insights web publication focuses on the results of the 2008 Faith Communities Today survey of congregations, and explores the issue of integrating new members into the life of the congregation.

Morgan, T., and Stevens, T. *Simply Strategic Volunteers: Empowering People for Ministry*. Loveland, CO: Group, 2005.

Ninety-nine ideas and strategies for involving and motivating volunteers into the life of your church.

Osborne, L. *Sticky Church*. Grand Rapids, MI: Zondervan, 2008.

What it takes to cultivate a "sticky" church and how to use the strategy of sermon-based small groups to retain members while leading your church into even deeper levels of discipleship.

Oswald, R. M., and Leas, S. B. *The Inviting Church: A Study of New Member Assimilation*. Washington, DC: Alban Institute, 1987.

Discover how your congregation can meet growth challenges. Includes a self-study design for assessing assimilation processes and analyzing visitors' perceptions.

Putnam, R. *Bowling Alone: The Collapse and Revival of American Community*. New York: Simon & Schuster, 2001.

Shows how we have become increasingly disconnected from family, friends, neighbors, and our democratic structures—and how we might reconnect.

Putnam, R., and Campbell, D. *American Grace: How Religion Divides and Unites Us*. New York: Simon & Schuster, 2010.

Includes a dozen in-depth profiles of diverse congregations across the country, which illuminate the trends described by the authors.

Putnam, R., and Feldstein, L. *Better Together: Restoring the American Community*. New York: Simon & Schuster, 2004.

Offers a hopeful message about civic renewal with stories of a dozen places around the country where people are engaging in new forms of social activism and community renewal.

Rauff, E. *Why People Join the Church: An Exploratory Study*. Nashville, TN: Glenmary Research, 1979.

A qualitative study of the stories of 180 men and women to discover how they came to join a church and the dynamics that were involved for each person.

Savage, J. *The Apathetic and Bored Church Member: Psychological and Theological Implications*. Pittsford, NY: Lead Consultants, 1976.
How people lose interest in being active church members and drift, and how to prevent this from happening.

Searcy, N., and Henson, J. *Fusion: Turning First-Time Guests into Fully-Engaged Members of Your Church*. Ventura, CA: Regal, 2008.
This practical guide offers a system used in Searcy's church, full of how-to steps and tools.

Shelley, M. (ed.). *Growing Your Church Through Training and Motivation: 30 Strategies to Transform Your Ministry*. Ada, MI: Bethany House, 1997.
How to equip and encourage your whole church for ministry. This book is full of reminders and suggestions that will help keep your church environment a healthy place for service.

Trumbauer, J. *Sharing the Ministry: A Practical Guide for Transforming Volunteers into Ministry (Stewardship)*. Minneapolis: Augsburg Fortress, 1995.
Educates parishioners on methods of placing gifts into action.

Waltz, M. *Lasting Impressions: From Visiting to Belonging*. Loveland, CO: Group, 2008.
Offering a proven strategy for turning church guests into believers, and believers into committed Christ-followers.

Wilson, M. *How to Mobilize Church Volunteers*. Minneapolis: Augsburg Fortress, 1983.
An authority in the field of volunteer management offers help with recruiting, training, and motivating people.

Winseman, A. *Growing an Engaged Church: How to Stop "Doing Church" and Start Being the Church Again*. New York: Gallup Press, 2007.
Based on solid research by the Gallup Organization, this book appeals to both Protestant and Catholic clergy and lay leaders who are looking for a way to bring more people to higher levels of engagement.

Wuthnow, R. *Loose Connections: Joining Together in America's Fragmented Communities*. Cambridge, MA: Harvard University Press, 1998.
The author argues that while certain kinds of civic engagement may be declining, innovative new forms are taking their place. People are still connected, but because of the realities of daily life, they form "loose connections."

● ● ●

For internet-based resources, see Appendix A. For books and other research related to the larger data groups referenced in this study, see Appendix B.

Acknowledgments

This book would not be possible without the bighearted help of many people.

Our families have been most gracious as we were away visiting churches, participating in conferences to discuss the research, or meeting with each other to crunch data and process the findings. They've also been great sounding boards at different points in the book's development. Thank you for putting up with our strange writing schedules, stressed deadlines, and odd fascination with percentages; for loving us through the entire process. We could not have finished this effort without your love and concern.

Our employers have been most generous in providing the time, computer software, professional memberships, and other resources that are necessary to pull together a book like this. We especially appreciate Leadership Network's funding, which enabled us to fly to different cities and do extended church visits for our interviews and field studies. We also received important guidance and administrative support from Dave Travis, Mark Sweeney, Greg Ligon, Stephanie Plagens, Kelly Kulesza, and Esther Thompson. Likewise we want to credit Hartford Seminary for Scott's sabbatical leave, and especially Hartford Institute for Religion Research colleagues David Roozen, Adair Lummis, Jim Nieman, and Sheryl Wiggins, who offered support, insights, data analysis, and valuable feedback along the way. Friends like Patrick Colgan, Kep James, Leonard Kageler, Paul D. Krampitz, and Hal Seed provided valuable insights in reading drafts of the book.

Our professional colleagues have been wonderful about sharing their research with us. We thank the various cohorts of Doctor of Ministry students at Hartford Seminary for raising the book's topic over and over again, with some acting as readers throughout the process. The Hartford Institute for Religion Research team provided access to twenty-five thousand parish inventory responses and the datasets associated with the Faith Community Today (FACT) project. A special thanks to Travis Lowe and Adair Lummis for their assistance with these multiple datasets. We especially appreciate Cynthia Woolever and Deborah Bruce, authors of A *Field Guide to U.S. Congregations* (second edition),* whose two waves of the U.S. Congregational Life Survey, with over one hundred thousand Protestant responses, set the pace in survey design and provided many points of comparison for our research.

The pastors, staff, and congregations at many churches gave us stories, insights, and access to both their victories and their challenges. We are indebted to the almost forty thousand people across twenty-five churches who let us study them in depth through a combination of congregational surveys and on-site visits (described further in Appendix B).

The team at Jossey-Bass has been a delight to work with. Our editor, Sheryl Fullerton, helped us in huge ways to develop and refine the concept that became this book's focus. We were assisted also by Alison Knowles, Jeff Wyneken, and Joanne Clapp Fullagar.

Finally we thank the readers of this book for taking bold steps of faith that involve a bigger view of their flocks in ways that strengthen and enlarge the Kingdom of God.

---

*See Appendix B.

The Authors

Scott Thumma, PhD, is a professor at Hartford Seminary and researcher at the Hartford Institute for Religion Research, Hartford, Connecticut (www.hartfordinstitute.org). His most recent book, *Beyond Megachurch Myth* (Jossey-Bass), coauthored with Dave Travis, documents his twenty years of studying the megachurch phenomenon. He has also researched and written on evangelicalism, the rise of nondenominational churches, the impact of the internet on church dynamics, and homosexuality and religious life. Scott is the director of the seminary's distance education program and codirector of the new Insights into Religion Portal (www.religioninsights.org) for the Lilly Endowment, as well as a consultant to churches and religious organizations on congregational vitality, planning, and new technologies. Scott and his family live in West Hartford, Connecticut.

Warren Bird, PhD, is director of research and intellectual capital development for Leadership Network (www.leadnet.org), a global ministry that accelerates the impact of high-capacity churches and their leaders. He is coauthor of twenty-two books on church leadership, two of them with Jossey-Bass: *Viral Churches: Helping Church Planters Become Movement Makers*, coauthored with Ed Stetzer; and *Culture Shift: Transforming Your Church from the Inside Out*, coauthored with Robert Lewis and Wayne Cordeiro. An ordained minister, he has served in various church staff positions for fifteen years. Since 1996 he has been an adjunct professor at Alliance Theological Seminary, Nyack and Manhattan, New York. Warren and his wife live in metro New York City.

Index

Page references followed by *fig* indicate an illustrated figure; followed by *t* indicate a table.

with no involvement, 36–37. *See also* Marginal involvement; 20 percent participants
80/20 Pareto Principle, 169–170
"Elevator speech," 50
Ephesians 4:11-13, 168
Estranged members: making the effort to bring them back, 115–116; marginal participation by, 36–37; reaching out to, 90–93

F
Facebook, 70, 147
FACT (Faith Communities Today 2008) research: on back-door hospitality, 90–91*fig*; on church characteristics and volunteer recruitment, 82–83*fig*; on church size and conflict patterns, 79; on clergy role in participation, 93; on multiple paths to assimilating people, 114; on positive factors of more-conservative churches, 80; on recognition of volunteers and future recruiting, 85*fig*–86; on roadblocks to member participation, 84*t*; on spiritual vitality impact of activities and programs, 90; on spiritually vital churches recruitment of volunteers, 81–82*fig*; on training volunteers and future recruiting, 86*t*; on volunteers and inviters, 87*fig*

Faith: "Aunt Susan" effect of differences in, 63; church growth through new expressions of, 161–162; cultural/social changed perception of, 61
1 Corinthians 12:27, 69
Funnel involvement models, 111–112

G
George, 32
Ginny, 110
Go to Meeting, 149
Goats and sheep, 41*t*
Good Shepherd's voice, 74
Groschel, Craig, 68
Guests. *See* Newcomers/guests

H
Hadaway, Kirk, 36, 37
Hartford Institute: parish inventory of, 19; parish profile recorded by, 170–171
High involvement participation: characteristics of, 5*t*, 6–9; commitment of, 4, 6; conflict patterns of, 14*fig*; continuum of, 5*t*; demographic patterns of, 12*fig*–13*fig*; listening team membership by, 41–42; listening to those engaged in, 1–2, 9–11; new role/responsibility correlation with, 15*t*–16; providing adequate personal rewards for, 10–11; similarities and differences of

those with, 11–14; spiritual life correlation to, 8–9t, 14–18; U.S. Congregational Life Survey on attitudes of, 9t. *See also* 20 percent participants; Voluntary participants

I

Increased participation: helping take the next step for, 18–20; listening team membership by those with, 42–43; listening to those moving toward, 11; multiple pathways to, 19t; new role or responsibility and, 15t
The indifferent members, 36–37
Individualized experience, 138–140
Infirm members: back-door hospitality to, 91; marginal participation by, 35
"Insights on Membership Commitment" (McMullen), 95
Interfaith marriages, 63
Inviters, 87*fig*
Involvement models: focusing on the 80 percent, 111–115; funnel approach of some, 111–112; meetings and big events, 109–110; membership first, 108; multiple stations, 109; newcomer classes—then options, 108–109; specific sequence, 109; training and serving, 110; typical linear and narrowing-path, 107; ultrasimplicity, 110

J

Jeannine, 91
Jenny, 101
John 10, 73

K

Karen, 92

L

Lapsed members: aged or infirm, 35, 91; back-door hospitality to, 90–93; estranged, 36–37, 90–93, 115–116; FACT survey on contacting, 90–91t; making the effort to bring them back, 115–116; networking to reach, 152–161. *See also* Uninvolved
Larger church survey: attenders versus staff on how to build involvement, 105t; description of, 5; on influence of relational connections on attendance, 112t–113; on initial invitation to church, 101t; on newcomers coming from another local church, 103t; staff versus attenders on reasons for continued attendance, 104t
Larger churches: Listening Teams for, 48–49; ways to increase member affiliation in, 77–79
Lasting Impressions: From Visiting to Belonging (Waltz), 31
Learning Teams: dealing with leadership challenges identified by, 123–124; description and goals of, 117–118; getting a

need for, 77–79; helping them use their gifts and interests, 136–138; inviters through, 87*fig*; recognition of, 85*fig*–86, 140–142; social changes impacting time for, 59–60, 62, 132, 137–138; spiritually vital churches' recruitment of, 81–82*fig*; training payoffs for, 86*t*, 135–136; worship format, church dynamics, and recruiting, 81–83*fig*. *See also* High involvement participation

W

Waltz, Mark, 31

Warren, 62, 107, 127, 165

Warren, Rick, 68, 69

Websites. *See* Church websites

Willow Creek's Reveal effort, 25

WORD, 170–171. *See also* Scripture teachings

Worship format: children involved in, 139–140; contemporary, 81; correlations between participation and, 146–147; exploring innovative approaches to, 161–163; virtual environment for, 147; volunteer recruitment and, 81–83*fig*. *See also* Church organization

Y

Yoido Full Gospel Church (Korea), 77

Other Books of Interest

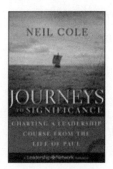

Journeys to Significance

Charting a Leadership Course from the Life of Paul

Neil Cole

Hardcover
ISBN: 978-1-118-00544-6

"This interpretive biography of Paul is a valuable resource for a leader who wants to pursue the *Leadership Mandate* (Hebrews 13:7-8) and learn from Paul's examples."

—Dr. J. Robert Clinton, Professor of Leadership,
School of Intercultural Studies, Fuller Theological Seminary

"The life and ministry of the apostle Paul prove a treasure trove for leaders' development when masterfully explored by Neil Cole. No matter what life/ministry phase you are in, you will find insights that help you better understand how you are being shaped for your leadership assignment."

—Reggie McNeal, author of *Missional Renaissance*,
The Present Future, and *A Work of Heart*

In *Journeys to Significance,* bestselling author and organic church leader Neil Cole takes us on a journey as we follow the life of the apostle Paul and learn valuable lessons about how God forms a leader over the course of his or her life. It's not about just reaching the end—it's about finishing well and keeping your eye on the ultimate goal, not on short-term wins or losses. *Journeys to Significance* provides valuable insights to help any leader (or aspiring leader) to build upon each journey so that finishing strong is not only possible, but is a clear and practical focus in the here and now.

NEIL COLE is an experienced and innovative church planter and pastor. He is the founder of the Awakening Chapels, which are reaching young postmodern people in urban settings, and a founder and executive director of Church Multiplication Associates. He is the author of several books including *Organic Church* and *Church 3.0,* both from Jossey-Bass.

Other Books of Interest

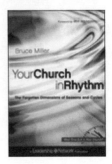

Your Church in Rhythm
The Forgotten Dimensions of Seasons and Cycles

Bruce Miller

Hardcover
ISBN: 978-0-470-94721-0

"One of the hardest places to find God's rhythm for life is in the church. It shouldn't be that way but it is. My good friend, Bruce Miller, has some ideas that can make the difference. For all those of you who have grown weary in well-doing, you can't afford not to read this important work."

—Randy Frazee, Senior Minister, Oak Hills Church in San Antonio, Texas; author of *Making Room for Life*

"How do you view a church as a living, dynamic organism? How do you discern and diagnose where it is in the 'life cycle' and how to treat it accordingly? *Your Church in Rhythm* is a look at how to see the church in a new way and wrestle with what to do given where it is. This work is well worth the time and reflection it will generate."

—Darrell Bock, Research Professor of New Testament and Professor of Spiritual Development and Culture, Dallas Theological Seminary

In *Your Church in Rhythm*, Bruce B. Miller introduces the concept of rhythm as a powerful approach to church life. Every ministry flows in rhythms in the stages of a church's life cycle and in regular cycles annually, monthly, weekly, but how can leaders maximize the God-given rhythms of life? Miller challenges the idea of a balanced church—trying to have it all, all the time. In place of the elusive search for balance, Miller proposes rhythm: flowing in seasons and cycles.

BRUCE B. MILLER is the founding and senior pastor of Christ Fellowship, formerly named McKinney Fellowship Bible Church, near Dallas, Texas. He also founded the Center for Church Based Training (CCBT) where he served for eleven years as the chairman of the Board of Directors. He speaks at conferences and seminars in the United States and other countries, including Mexico, China, Switzerland, Austria, and Germany.

Other Books of Interest

Cracking Your Church's Culture Code
Seven Keys to Unleashing Vision & Inspiration

Samuel R. Chand

Hardcover
ISBN: 978-0-470-57230-6

"*Cracking Your Church's Culture Code* provides a methodical introduction to understanding the idiosyncratic dynamics of your church and its impact on the overall vision of your ministry. This book is comprehensible and constructive as it reveals the seven important keys to creating a cohesive tone within your organization."

—Bishop T. D. Jakes, The Potter's House of Dallas

"Dr. Chand said, 'Culture—not vision or strategy--is the most powerful factor in any organization.' I couldn't agree more. Dr. Chand's latest book, *Cracking Your Church's Culture Code*, is a must-read for every church leader. If you want your ministry to move forward, buy this book for everyone on your leadership team!"

—Craig Groeschel, Senior Pastor of LifeChurch.tv, author of *The Christian Atheist*

Why is it that the best strategic plans and good leadership often are not able to move churches in the desired direction? Sam Chand contends that toxic culture is to blame. Quite often, leaders don't sense the toxicity, but it poisons their relationships and derails their vision. This work describes five easily identifiable categories of church culture (inspiring-accepting-stagnant-discouraging-toxic), with diagnostic descriptions in the book and a separate online assessment tool. The reader will be able to identify strengths and needs of their church's culture, and then apply practical strategies (communication, control and authority, selection and placement of personnel, etc.) to make their church's culture more positive.

DR. SAM CHAND is a leadership consultant and coach who works with a variety of church leaders and speaks regularly at leadership and ministerial conferences, churches, corporations, seminars and in other leadership development settings. He has served on the board of EQUIP (Dr. John Maxwell's ministry), equipping five million leaders world-wide, and has coached many influential leaders.

Other Books of Interest

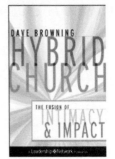

Hybrid Church
The Fusion of Intimacy & Impact

Dave Browning

Hardcover
ISBN: 978-0-470-57230-6

"A really well-articulated, organizationally insightful, insider's view of what happens when missional meets mega and when movemental forms engage best practice in contemporary church leadership and organization."
—**Alan Hirsch**, director, Future Travelers; author, *The Forgotten Ways*; and coauthor, *On the Verge*

"Dave Browning understands that accomplishing big dreams requires small actions. In *Hybrid Church* you get practical first-hand experience in blending the megachurch and the microchurch into a consistent ministry philosophy... *Hybrid Church* is a must-read for leaders who want to hear from someone who is really getting it done in big and small ways!"
—**Dave Ferguson**, lead pastor, Community Christian Church, and movement leader, NewThing

Hybrid Church is a practical guide for clergy and leaders who want to have the intimacy of small "house church" groups and the impact of very large megachurches. Pastor Dave Browning explains, the small church has the advantage of harnessing the power of prayer in intimate groups, focusing on Christ-centeredness, and offering comfortableness, while megachurches tap into the strength of faith, momentum, and creativity. By combining all these advantages into a hybrid church, leaders and their churches can reach more people more effectively. Ultimately, this vision of a hybrid church is not about numbers, it is about people. It is about fulfilling the great commission and bringing people out of darkness into God's marvelous light.

DAVE BROWNING is a visionary minimalist and the founder of Christ the King Community Church, International (CTK). CTK is a nondenominational, multilocation church that has been noted as one of the "fastest growing" and "most innovative" churches in America by employing the K.I.S.S method: "keep it simple and scalable." It involves 17,000 people in several countries. He is the author of *Deliberate Simplicity: How the Church Does More by Doing Less*.